ALICIA KEYS HAS WON 15 GRAMMYS AND SOLD MORE THAN 40 MILLION ALBUMS, MAKING HER ONE OF THE MOST POPULAR ARTISTS OF THE 21ST CENTURY.

ARETHA FRANKLIN

JAY-Z

ED SHEERAN

FOR MORE INFORMATION ON THESE STARS
FROM MUSIC HISTORY:
ALICIA KEYS, PREVIOUS PAGE: SEE PAGE 169
ARETHA FRANKLIN: SEE PAGE 119
ED SHEERAN: SEE PAGE 156
JAY-Z: SEE PAGE 152
SPICE GIRLS: SEE PAGE 168
DIZZY GILLESPIE: SEE PAGE 105
ADELE: SEE PAGE 157

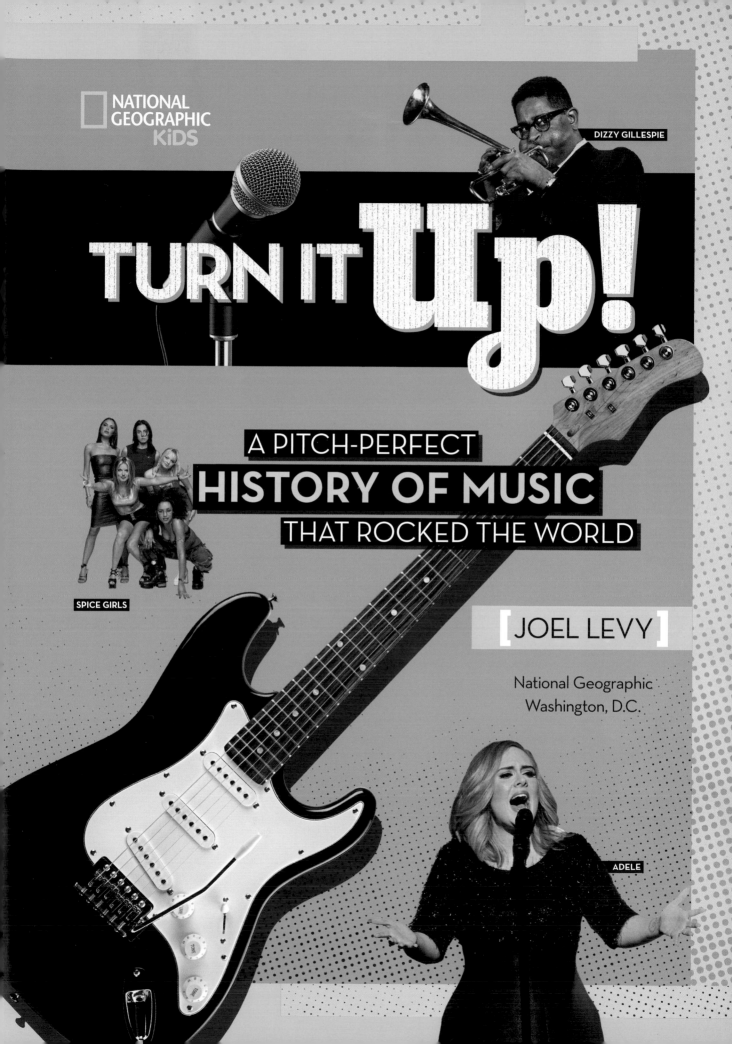

NATIONAL GEOGRAPHIC KiDS

DIZZY GILLESPIE

TURN IT UP!

A PITCH-PERFECT
HISTORY OF MUSIC
THAT ROCKED THE WORLD

SPICE GIRLS

[JOEL LEVY]

National Geographic
Washington, D.C.

ADELE

Contents

LUDWIG VAN BEETHOVEN

Introduction 6
Mastering Music 8

[CHAPTER **One**]

The Earliest Tunes 10

Play Those Bones 12
Making Medieval Music 14
Majestic Melodies 16
So Noted 18
Gongs of the Gamelan 20
Renaissance Rhythms 22
Big and Baroque 24
Creating Instrumentals 26
He's Bach, Baby 28
Hark! A Harpsichord! 30
More Musical Masters 32

[CHAPTER **Two**]

Isn't It Romantic... 34

Orchestrating Orchestras 36
Maximum Mozart 38
Chamber Music 40
The Best of Beethoven 42
Isn't It Romantic? 44
Totally Talented 46
The Outstanding Orchestra 48
Symphonic Shifts 50
The Wonder Women of
   Classical Music 52
Notes of Pride 54
Only in America 56
Strike Up the Band! 58
Opening Up to Opera 60
The Many Moods of Asian Opera 62
More Musical Masters 64

[CHAPTER **Three**]

Thoroughly Modern Music 66

New Century, New Start 68
Riot at the Ballet 70
The Spirit of Spain
   and Latin America 72
Anything Goes in America 74
Gotta Sing, Gotta Dance! 76
That's So Country 78
Musical Mania 80
The Great American Songbook 82
Songs of the Silver Screen 84
More Musical Masters 86

[CHAPTER **Four**]

All-American Sound 88

Spirited Singing 90
Ragged Time Rhythms 92
Belt Out Those Blues 94
A Jazzy Start 96
Really Big Bands 98
Swing Sets 100
Era of the Big Bands 102
Boppin' to Bebop 104
The Sound of Cool 106
Free From Rules 108
Funky Fusions 110
More Musical Masters 112

BEIJING OPERA PERFORMER

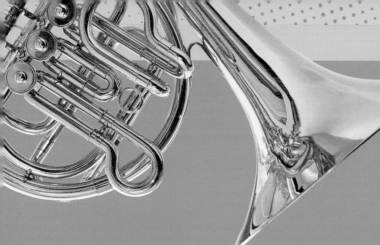

CHUCK BERRY

[CHAPTER **Five**]

Play It Loud 114

We've Got the Blues   116
Giving Praise   118
Everybody Rock!   120
Folksy Protests   122
Rocking the Greatest Stage   124
The British Are Coming!   126
Rocking the Blues   128
Get Funky   130
Sitar Stars   132
Rock Styles   134
Irresistible Indipop   136
More Musical Masters   138

[CHAPTER **Six**]

Pop Goes the Music 140

Reggae Rhythms   142
Metalheads   144
Such a Punk   146
What's Your Tribe?   148
Sisters Start Doin' It
    for Themselves   150
Get Hip with the Beat   152
Run-DMC Rock the House   154
Stadium Superstars   156
All In on Afropop   158
Less Is More   160
Dance to the Music   162

More Musical Masters   164
Rockin' Country   166
Girl Power   168
Let's Hear It for Boy Bands! 170
They've Got Talent   172
Cue Up the K-pop   174
Breaking the Mold   176
Full Stream Ahead   178
More Musical Masters   180

Timeline   182
Glossary   184
Further Reading & Resources 186
Index   187
Illustration Credits   191

JUSTIN
TIMBERLAKE

JANELLE MONÁE

Introduction

AS PLATO ONCE SAID:

"Music gives a soul to the universe, wings to the mind, flight to the imagination, and life to everything."

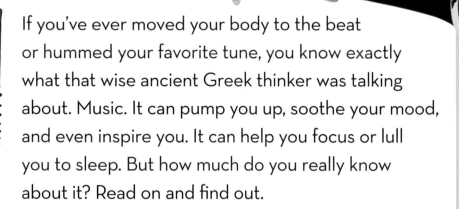

If you've ever moved your body to the beat or hummed your favorite tune, you know exactly what that wise ancient Greek thinker was talking about. Music. It can pump you up, soothe your mood, and even inspire you. It can help you focus or lull you to sleep. But how much do you really know about it? Read on and find out.

KEEP YOUR EARS OPEN FOR THESE BONUS TRACKS:

AWESOME INSTRUMENT
Don't know your sax from your sousaphone? These boxes explain important instruments, where they came from, and how they work.

TUNEFUL TERMS
Music and its history are full of names and terms, some of which may be unfamiliar. These boxes explain important tidbits you need to know.

MUSICAL MASTER
Learn more about musical maestros from these boxes. Each tells you about an important person and explains why their music matters.

SYNTHESIZER

EGYPTIAN LYRE

LADY GAGA

BILLIE HOLIDAY

Mozart wrote his first symphony at only eight years old. Bruno Mars was once the youngest Elvis impersonator in Hawaii. Your parents' taste in music might influence yours. (Sorry, it's true.)

This book doesn't just explain the history of music. It shows how different types of music are related, and why some artists sing or play in certain styles. Discover beats and rhythms you've never even heard about, from ragtime to rock steady to highlife.

Ever wonder what kind of music our prehistoric ancestors enjoyed? Or how music has influenced history? Who knew the ancient Greeks are connected to Beyoncé by way of Beethoven? The story of music is as catchy and memorable as the latest No. 1 hit, and as old as humanity itself. With so much time and space to cover, it would be impossible to fit it all in one book! So, think of this as a generous sampling of some key moments and performers in music history to get your ears tuned and your toes tapping. Feel free to sing along.

The name Imagine Dragons is an anagram, but only the band members know what it is!

IMAGINE DRAGONS

BEHIND THE NOTES
The story of music is about so much more than notes on a page. These boxes explore the many worlds connected to music and tell the fascinating stories behind the tunes.

LISTEN UP!
Every spread includes one essential piece you might want to listen to. Remember to check with a grown-up before looking up any songs online.

THE BEATLES

BEIJING OPERA

Mastering Music

SIMPLY PUT, MUSIC IS THE PLEASING ARRANGEMENT OF NOTES. But who decides what makes them pleasing? Every culture has its own forms of music—its own sounds, styles, and traditions. Music might be used for religious services or to add depth and feeling to other art forms (what's a movie without a great soundtrack?). Or it might be purely for fun. At the most basic level, all music works in the same way with the same key elements: pitch, melody, and rhythm.

VIBRATING GUITAR STRING

SOUND WAVES

We hear music the way that we hear all noise: as sound waves. A sound wave is the movement of air caused when something vibrates, such as an instrument or a speaker in a sound system. The vibration moves the air particles around it, which pass the vibration on to the particles next to them, and on and on. Our ears detect this movement as sound.

PITCH AND FREQUENCY

The pitch of a note is how high or low it sounds. When a sound wave vibrates a lot each second, it makes a high note. When a sound wave vibrates only a few times a second, it makes a low note. This is called the frequency of the sound wave. The higher the frequency, the higher the note. The frequency of a sound wave can be drawn as a wavy line—the closer together the peaks of the line are, the higher the frequency and the higher the pitch.

LOWER NOTES   HIGHER NOTES

? DID YOU KNOW?

Frequency is measured in Hertz (Hz), named after the German scientist Heinrich Hertz, who first showed that sound waves exist. Humans can hear sounds between 20 Hz (very low frequency) and 20,000 Hz (very high). Many animals, such as dogs, can hear frequencies much higher than that.

[NOTES]

Musical notes are divided into groups called scales. A lot of Western music is based on the chromatic scale, which has 12 notes. On a keyboard, these notes are arranged in repeating patterns of seven white notes and five black notes. This pattern is known as an octave—from the Latin word for "eighth"—because the pattern repeats after every seventh white note.

AN OCTAVE ON A KEYBOARD

C# D# F# G# A#
Db Eb Gb Ab Bb

C D E F G A B

[RHYTHM]

The rhythm is the feel or pulse of the music—the part that gets your foot tapping and your body rocking. Rhythm is a combination of several musical elements: how many beats (or pulses) are in each part of music, the speed the beats are played at, how many beats each note is played for, the rests between the notes, and the pattern of beats.

DOUBLE BASS

DJEMBE DRUMMER

[MELODY]

The melody is the specific order of the musical notes that make up the tune of a song—the part you sing along to. Most Western music is based on melody. Classical music pieces may have several melodies: a main melody, or theme, and a number of variations of the theme. Pop and folk music are usually simpler. Jazz musicians often improvise new melodies based on existing tunes.

[HARMONY]

Harmony is the combination of two or more notes. Three or more notes played together make up a chord. A lot of modern Western music, including classical, pop, and jazz, features a melody sung or played on top of sequences of chords (known as chord progressions), which creates a harmony.

A PROCESSION OF ANCIENT MAYA MUSICIANS,
PAINTED ABOUT A.D. 790 IN BONAMPAK, MEXICO

The Earliest
Tunes

F or as long as we've been around to enjoy it, music has been a part of human history. We play music to tell stories, for religious reasons, and often just for fun. Thousands of years ago, ancient peoples invented all kinds of musical instruments and figured out that math and music are related (see p. 13). By the late 15th century, however, music was changing like never before. Beginning in the 1600s, the Baroque era delivered the first operas, overtures, and concertos, and it gave us complex and beautiful music that's still played today.

Play Those **Bones**

THE FIRST MUSICAL INSTRUMENT WAS THE HUMAN VOICE.
The earliest singers—we're talking between 50,000 and 200,000 years ago—probably clapped their hands or banged rocks to keep the beat. The first known musical instruments date back about 40,000 years. And you thought your school's marching band instruments were old! Flutes made of bones were discovered in caves in Germany. They are so old we don't know whether humans or our earlier ancestors, such as the Neanderthal people, played them.

Early music may have had links to religious rituals. An ancient flute carved from the bones of a vulture was discovered near a statue of a goddess. It's even believed that music might have helped modern humans survive better than our ancestors because performing rituals and songs helped people communicate and work together.

Carvings and texts from ancient Assyria and Egypt show harps, flutes, and string instruments. The ancient Chinese classified their instruments by the material they were made with: silk, bamboo, hide, clay, metal, stone, or wood. They may have been the first ancient peoples to divide instruments into groups as we do today.

In ancient Greece, the most popular instrument was the lyre, a type of small harp. Performers would sing long epic poems while playing the phorminx, a four-stringed lyre. The Greeks tended to prefer music accompanied by lyrics, so they liked musicians to play a stringed instrument, such as a lyre, freeing up their mouths to sing. Music, especially sung words, was also important to their theater. At least one ancient play written in the fifth century B.C. by the poet and playwright Euripides includes sung music.

In ancient Egypt, dancers and flute players often accompanied work, such as planting crops.

◄ BONE FLUTE

AN EGYPTIAN DOUBLE FLUTE PLAYER, PAINTED ON A TOMB ABOUT 1390 B.C.

+ AWESOME INSTRUMENT +
LYRE

WITH ITS TWO ARMS, TUNING PEGS, A TAILPIECE, AND SEVEN STRINGS, the lyre looks a lot like a modern harp. Its strings are all the same length but are in different thicknesses. A musician strums or plucks the strings to play, using a plectrum (a small flat piece of hard material). According to ancient Greek myth, the Greek god Hermes made the first lyre from the shell of a tortoise and some reeds.

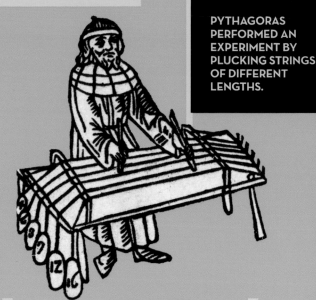

PYTHAGORAS PERFORMED AN EXPERIMENT BY PLUCKING STRINGS OF DIFFERENT LENGTHS.

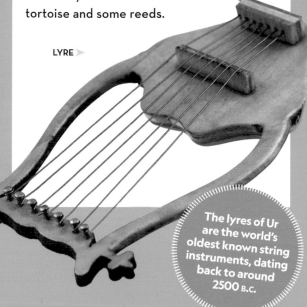

LYRE ➤

The lyres of Ur are the world's oldest known string instruments, dating back to around 2500 B.C.

[BEHIND the Notes]

The ancient Greek philosopher Pythagoras is said to be the first to work out music's mathematical equation. He determined how notes relate to one another and saw that the note a string plays is related to how long the string is. Pythagoras thought that the planets made a kind of music based on these rules. The Christian philosopher St. Augustine (4th–5th century A.D.) believed that when a person dies, he or she hears that music.

LISTEN UP!
MICHAEL LEVY, "HURRIAN HYMN H6"

[BEHIND the Notes]

Ancient peoples around the world had different explanations for where music came from. The ancient Egyptians believed that the goddess Hathor invented music. An ancient Chinese legend says that music was invented by an old man named Ling Lun, who made bamboo pipes tuned to the songs of birds. The ancient Greeks thought the god Hermes invented the lyre. In another Greek myth, Orpheus was a musician who sang and played music so beautifully that even animals were charmed by him.

THE GREEK MUSICIAN ORPHEUS PLAYING A LYRE

13

Making
Medieval Music

TODAY, YOU CAN HEAR ANY KIND OF MUSIC FROM ANY PART OF THE WORLD with the touch of a screen. But most ancient people only knew the music of the region where they lived. When people began to travel more, they took their music on the road with them. Before long, ancient Greek music had evolved into Roman music, which eventually led to medieval Western music. Other regions, such as India and Mexico, also had strong musical traditions that were completely separate from European music.

Although it is difficult for us to know what the music of the ancients sounded like, they used music much like we do today: as entertainment, in religious ceremonies, and in drama. Greek ideas concerning musical scales, called modes, were passed to the Romans and medieval Europeans. Early medieval music was monophonic, meaning it did not use harmonies.

In medieval India, Hindu music was used for religious ceremonies and plays. The music was complex and included harps and lutes, which were eventually replaced by a long-necked string instrument called a stick zither in about A.D. 700.

The Aztec had a special word for music, *cuicatlamatiliztli,* which means the "art of song." Aztec musicians "sang" on their instruments and when they danced, they "sang with the feet." The Aztec played clay flutes, trumpets made from conch shells, and wooden drums.

AZTEC PLAYING TEPONAZTLI AND HUEHUETL DRUMS IN THE 1500s

The word "music" comes from the Greek word *mousike,* which means "art of the muses."

14   **A HINDU PERCUSSIONIST**

[TUNEFUL **Terms**

Poets and musicians from southern France were called troubadours. The name came from the French word, *trouver*, or to find, because these musicians found or invented poems and melodies. The troubadours sang and danced, accompanied by the lute and shawm (an instrument like an oboe). They sang about love, life at the royal courts, and stories about famous people, such as King Arthur.

THE NOBLEWOMAN CASTELLOZA WAS A FEMALE TROUBADOUR, OR TROBAIRITZ. ONLY THREE OF HER SONGS SURVIVE.

 **LISTEN UP!**
KATHRYN TICKELL, "LADS OF ALNWICK"

The art of the troubadours died out around the time of the Black Death plague in 1348.

[BEHIND **the Notes**

The emperor Nero, who ruled Rome from A.D. 54 to 68, was famous for his love of music. It is said that he trained for six years before he was willing to perform in public competitions. He was also careful about the food he ate and did special exercises to strengthen his singing voice. Legend has it that while a great fire destroyed much of Rome in A.D. 64, Nero played music—leading to the accusation that he "fiddled while Rome burned."

NERO WAS ACCUSED OF STARTING THE GREAT FIRE OF ROME TO CLEAR SPACE FOR A NEW PALACE.

+ AWESOME INSTRUMENT +
HORNPIPE

A HORNPIPE IS AN AEROPHONE INSTRUMENT; it makes a sound when air vibrates inside it. The bell of the instrument is made of horn and fits into one end of a hollow stick, which makes the sound louder. A drawing of a hornpipe was discovered in a Mediterranean tomb from 1400 B.C. The bagpipe, a popular instrument in medieval times, is two or more hornpipes attached to one bag. Made from animal skin, the bag lets air flow evenly when it's played.

BAGPIPE ➤

15

Majestic Melodies

MOST MAJOR RELIGIONS RELY ON MUSIC AND SINGING TO REFLECT SPIRITUAL BELIEFS as well as to help prepare people for worship. However, songs and chants aren't just nice to listen to. They can make it easier to learn and recite prayers and teachings. Whether it's the uplifting, powerful voices of a gospel choir, the ritual chanting of Buddhist monks, or the simple soothing sounds of guitar, music has long played a role in religious practices.

The record for the longest nonstop chant is 24 hours 10 minutes, set in 2015 at a Hindu temple in Texas, U.S.A.

THESE 15TH-CENTURY MUSLIMS ARE SUFI DERVISHES. THEIR ENERGETIC DANCING WAS A WAY TO MEDITATE.

In medieval Europe, just about the only music in churches was a type of singing called plainsong, in which singers chanted words without instrumental backing—it is sometimes also called plainchant. Plainsong is a beautiful form of sacred music that's used all over the world.

Chanting is an important part of Buddhism, too, because it helps worshippers to meditate and focus. One well-known Buddhist chant is the Sanskrit line *Om mani padme hum*. The basic English translation is, "Hail the jewel in the lotus," but each part of the chant has a special meaning to Buddhists.

India has many different kinds of religious music. Hindus sing bhajans, or songs that help worshippers get closer to their gods. During the singing of the South Asian poetic hymns called qawwali, worshippers chant until they fall into a blissful, trancelike state.

A BUDDHIST MONK CHANTS.

In Judaism, religious music includes cantillation (the chanting of readings from the Bible), the chanting of prayers, and synagogue song. Islamic classical music started around A.D. 700 in Syria and later Iraq, with different types of songs, such as the *al-ghina' ar-raqiq*, or "gentle song." They used instruments such as the oud (lute), the duff (frame drum), and the qadib (percussion stick).

TUNEFUL **Terms**

Churches played a key role in the development of Western music in medieval Europe. In the ninth century, people started to sing music with more than one melodic line sounding together, called polyphony. When extra voices were added to plainsong, the new style was called organum.

BEAUTIFULLY ILLUSTRATED SHEET MUSIC FOR A TYPE OF PLAINSONG CALLED GREGORIAN CHANT

BEHIND **the Notes**

The adhan is the Islamic call to prayer and is sung from the mosque five times a day. The person who sings the adhan is a muezzin, or prayer caller. In the Middle Ages, bands sometimes accompanied the muezzin. The adhan varies, but it is always sounded once from a mosque's minaret (tower) and then again inside the mosque.

A MUEZZIN CALLING MUSLIMS TO PRAYER FROM THE MINARET OF A MOSQUE

A Muslim tradition is to sing the adhan into the ear of a newborn baby.

 **LISTEN UP!**

ETIENNE DE LIEGE, "INVITATORIUM: DEUM VERUM"

TUNEFUL **Terms**

A hymn is a song of praise. In the Catholic Church, priests and choirs traditionally sang hymns in Latin, but churchgoers couldn't join in. Martin Luther, who in 1567 began the religious movement to reform the Catholic Church known as the Reformation, wanted hymns to be sung in the language of ordinary people so that everyone would understand them and anyone could belt them out loudly.

MARTIN LUTHER

17

So Noted

AS THE SIMPLE MUSIC OF THE MEDIEVAL PERIOD BECAME MORE COMPLICATED, musicians began to need a system to write their music down. Eventually, notation developed. That meant composers could both preserve their work and share it with others, and more people could enjoy it. Today, we can play music that's several hundred years old because of notation. We can also write our own music for others to perform some time in the future.

In 2017, Audrey Luna hit the highest note ever sung at New York City's Metropolitan Opera—an A above high C.

In about A.D. 1300, musicians in France and Italy began creating a new type of music known as New Art. They used repeated patterns of sound, also known as rhythms, as well as chords, or several different notes that complement each other when they're played at the same time.

Around the same time that rhythms and chords were developing, the system for writing down music was changing. Before then, monks had written signs called neumes above the words of a plainsong to show whether a note should be high or low, but the monks didn't specify exact notes or rhythms. In about A.D. 1000, an Italian monk named Guido d'Arezzo decided to write his notes on a staff, which is a set of special lines that let a composer specify the pitch—the highness or lowness of a sound. Then a French composer named Guillaume de Machaut started to use symbols to show how long each note should be played. By about 1600, musicians were writing notes that looked pretty much like today's system.

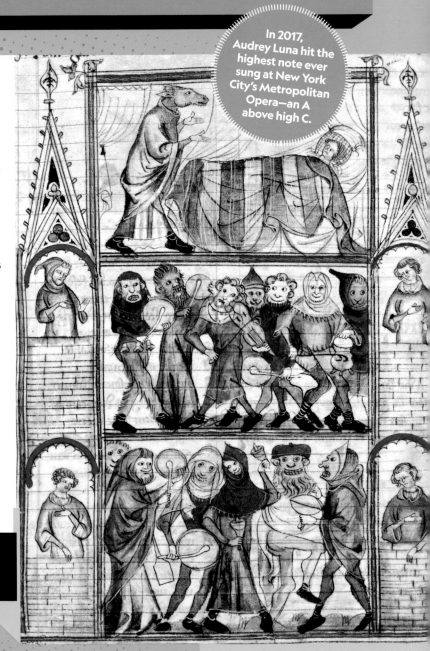

THIS ILLUSTRATED POEM FROM 1316, "THE ROMANCE OF FAUVEL," SHOWS A PROCESSION OF MEDIEVAL MUSICIANS.

★

+ MUSICAL MASTER +

+ GUILLAUME + DE MACHAUT

Guillaume de Machaut was a 14th-century French poet and musician. He wrote many songs and music for a Christian prayer service, which was an important type of music at the time. He was the King of Bohemia's traveling buddy, and together they went around discovering new kinds of music.

TUNEFUL Terms

Have you ever sung a song in a round with a big group of people? First, one group sings a line, then the next group starts singing the same line a few beats later, and on and on. When it works, it creates an amazing echoing effect. When it doesn't, it's a wall of noise. The medieval term for a round is "rota," which means singing in the round. One famous rota is the French song "Frère Jacques."

THE SHEET MUSIC FOR A FAMOUS ENGLISH ROTA FROM THE 1200s, "SUMMER IS COMING"

A line in "Summer Is Coming" translates into modern English as "The bullock stirs, the goat toots."

 LISTEN UP!
THE HILLIARD ENSEMBLE, "SUMER IS ICUMEN IN" ("SUMMER IS COMING")

[BEHIND the Notes]

Today, most musicians write down their music on staff paper. At the beginning of the staff, on the left-hand side, is a symbol called a clef, which shows the range of notes written on all of the staves, or lines. The individual notes are marked on the staves. Like any alphabet, certain markings indicate certain notes. Each note has a note value that is counted in beats. A quarter note lasts for one beat, a half note for two beats, a whole note for four beats, and so on.

CLEFS AND MUSICAL NOTES

TREBLE CLEF

BASS CLEF

QUARTER NOTE (1 BEAT)

HALF NOTE (2 BEATS)

EIGHTH NOTE (½ BEAT)

SIXTEENTH NOTE (¼ BEAT)

WHOLE NOTE (4 BEATS)

Gongs of the Gamelan

A GAMELAN IS A TRADITIONAL INDONESIAN ORCHESTRA, immediately recognizable because of the beautiful sound of the metal instruments at its heart. Gamelans developed on the islands of Indonesia in the Middle Ages, bringing together local beliefs and musical traditions with instruments from mainland Asia, such as gongs. This gamelan orchestra from the island of Bali is playing at a wedding. Indonesians believe the music is guided by spirits, so it is played for both religious reasons and entertainment.

PLAYING THE VIBES
Metallophones are similar to xylophones, but with metal bars instead of wooden ones.

CYMBAL SOUNDS
Balinese gamelans use metal cymbals to make rattling sounds. Cymbals are not usually found in Javanese gamelans.

GONGING UP Gongs, usually made of bronze, are the most important instrument in the gamelan.

MORE METALLOPHONES
In a Balinese gamelan, like this one, there are usually more metallophones than gongs.

FOOT LOOSE As a sign of respect for the spirits that guide the gamelan, musicians take off their shoes and play barefoot.

DIFFERENT STROKES
Different size gongs will give different notes when hit.

Renaissance **Rhythms**

THE RENAISSANCE, FOLLOWING THE MIDDLE AGES, WAS A GOLDEN AGE FOR ART AND MUSIC IN EUROPE. While Leonardo da Vinci was painting his masterpiece "Mona Lisa," great musicians and composers such as William Byrd and Giovanni Pierluigi da Palestrina were busy creating music for different instruments, composing songs and dances, and inventing new styles of music. The Renaissance introduced new ways of writing, playing, and even listening to music.

The Renaissance began in the 15th century and ended around 1600. Starting in Italy, it spread across Europe. Italian Renaissance musicians wrote songs called madrigals, which had lines for several voices and were mostly sung without instruments (unaccompanied). Singers performed madrigals all over Europe. The English loved composing madrigals, especially versions that wove a lot of voices around each other. These lively songs sounded full and fast and had an energetic "texture."

Songs were played by groups of musicians known as consorts. These consorts might have featured a lute (see p. 23), a virginal (a kind of harpsichord), a viol (a violin played like a cello), or a sackbut (an early trombone). Around this time, composers also started writing instrumentals—music for instruments without a voice accompaniment. They tended to emphasize the various sounds that instruments can make.

The "fa la la" refrain in the Christmas carol "Deck the Halls" was taken from a madrigal.

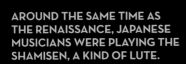

AROUND THE SAME TIME AS THE RENAISSANCE, JAPANESE MUSICIANS WERE PLAYING THE SHAMISEN, A KIND OF LUTE.

A VIRGINAL OWNED BY QUEEN ELIZABETH I OF ENGLAND ➤

Da Palestrina was a busy man—he composed more than 100 masses, 70 hymns, and 140 madrigals.

+ MUSICAL MASTERS +

+ DA PALESTRINA, + TALLIS, AND BYRD

Italian Renaissance composer Giovanni Pierluigi da Palestrina is best remembered for establishing new rules for music that made it more exciting and easier to listen to. He insisted that music should always flow, and that there should only be small jumps between the notes of melodies. Two English composers named Thomas Tallis and William Byrd, who worked at the court of Queen Elizabeth I, were celebrated for their madrigals and church music. At the time, they were the only two people in England granted a license to print and publish their music.

GIOVANNI PIERLUIGI DA PALESTRINA

+ AWESOME INSTRUMENT + LUTE

A LUTE IS A WOODEN STRING INSTRUMENT THAT'S RELATED TO THE GUITAR. In Renaissance Europe, lutes had a teardrop-shaped body, a flat front, and a curved back. The strings ran along the neck, which bent backward. The neck had marks called frets, which showed players where to put their fingers. The European lute developed from the oud, a string instrument which was first brought to Spain by the nomadic Moors of northern Africa.

◄ RENAISSANCE LUTE

[BEHIND the Notes]

The printing press was invented by the German Johannes Gutenberg around 1450. He introduced "movable type," separate metal pieces with alphabet letters and characters that could be rearranged. This invention had a huge impact on music, because many more people now had access to composers' works. The first printed book that included music was the *Mainz Psalter*, printed in 1457. The staves were printed by a printing press, while the rest of the music was written in by hand. By the 1520s, all the elements of the music could be printed together.

THE MAINZ PSALTER

LISTEN UP!
THOMAS TALLIS, "TALLIS' CANON"

Big and **Baroque**

BEGINNING AROUND 1600, THE BAROQUE MUSICAL ERA BEGAN, AND IT WOULD LAST UNTIL ABOUT 1750. Named after a Portuguese word that describes a heavily decorated piece of jewelry, Baroque music was both beautiful and complicated. The term is also used to describe art and architecture of the time. Baroque-era composers created the first operas, along with many other types of choral music (music written for a choir). A lot of Baroque music is still widely performed today.

CLAUDIO MONTEVERDI

Baroque composers further developed notation by adding instructions for a note's pitch—whether it should sound higher or lower. They used symbols called sharps and flats that were written next to a note on a staff. A sharp raises the pitch of a note a half step while a flat lowers the pitch of a note a half step.

In the Baroque period, a new singing style known as recitative began in Florence, Italy. Singers spoke (or recited) certain lines and sang others, all while a low instrument, such as a cello, played in the background. Known as a bass line, this background music became a major feature of the Baroque style. The world's first great opera, *L'Orfeo*, by Italian composer Claudio Monteverdi, also debuted around this time. Operas tell stories through singing, acting, instrumentals, and dancing, featuring solos called arias for star performers.

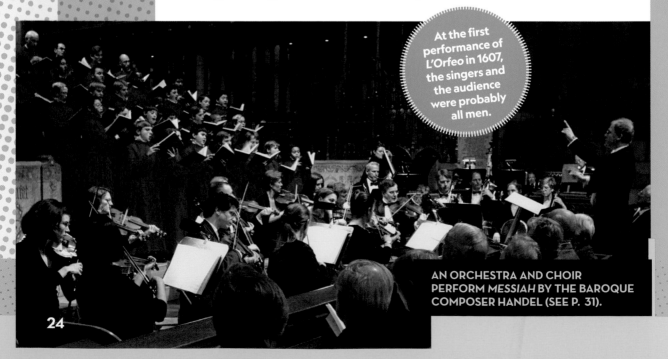

At the first performance of *L'Orfeo* in 1607, the singers and the audience were probably all men.

AN ORCHESTRA AND CHOIR PERFORM *MESSIAH* BY THE BAROQUE COMPOSER HANDEL (SEE P. 31).

[TUNEFUL **Terms**]

KING LOUIS XIV OF FRANCE

The overture, a piece of music played by an orchestra before an opera or ballet, first evolved during the Baroque era. Italian composer Alessandro Scarlatti created unique overtures that switched from fast to slow to fast. Later composers copied his idea. In the French court of Louis XIV, Jean-Baptiste Lully (see p. 33) wrote overtures that started slow, then got even slower. These were followed by dances in which the king himself sometimes took part.

+ MUSICAL MASTER +

+ HENRY PURCELL +

English composer Henry Purcell was considered to be one of the finest composers of the Baroque period. He was the organist at the Chapel Royal and wrote music that mixed French and Italian styles with traditional English folk songs. Purcell is best known for his opera *Dido and Aeneas*, based on the ancient Roman myth, but he also wrote pieces for royal birthdays and funerals. Purcell died young at just 36 years old.

Pete Townshend, of the rock band The Who, claimed Purcell's harmonies were an influence on his music.

LISTEN UP!
JEAN-BAPTISTE LULLY, "MARCHE POUR LE CÉRÉMONIE DES TURCS"

[BEHIND **the Notes**]

A person who pays composers to write music is called a patron. Composers often earned their living when royal families across Europe became their patrons. Kings and queens competed to get the best composers to work for them. In 1694, the English composer Henry Purcell wrote music for the funeral procession of Queen Mary II.

QUEEN MARY II'S FUNERAL PROCESSION THROUGH LONDON

Creating
Instrumentals

INSTRUMENTS WERE JUST AS IMPORTANT AS VOICES TO THE BAROQUE STYLE. Orchestras made up mostly of string instruments got bigger. And new styles of instrumental music were invented, using strong tunes, contrasts, and extra notes called ornaments. People loved the dramatic style, and audiences still enjoy a lot of Baroque pieces today. If you've ever seen an orchestra play online, at your school, or at a live performance, you may have felt the excitement of watching so many instruments making a single piece of music.

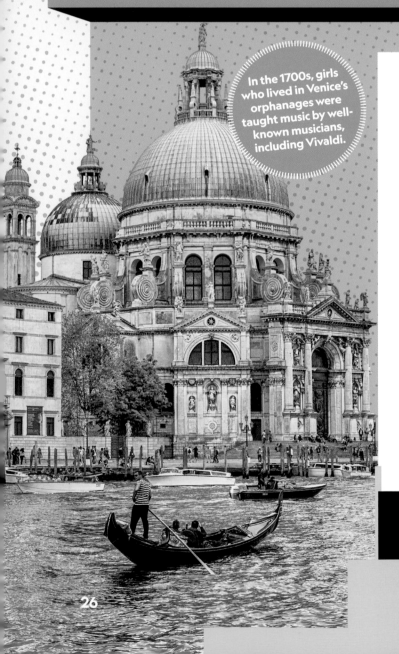

In the 1700s, girls who lived in Venice's orphanages were taught music by well-known musicians, including Vivaldi.

Baroque composers were continually developing new types of music. One kind, called a toccata, had musicians move their fingers really fast on a keyboard or string instrument. Another type, called a fantasia, used contrast. First, one instrument (or voice) would play a few notes, also called a phrase of music. Then other instruments would either echo the phrase or change it a little. A third new type of music, called a fugue, used a theme that repeated all the way through a piece.

Baroque composers also wrote suites, which were collections of dance music linked together, and concertos, a word that comes from the Latin for "get together." The first concertos were performed in large churches in Venice, Italy, and featured several choruses. The instruments seemed to play and respond to each other, as though they were having a conversation through song.

CONCERTOS ARE STILL PERFORMED AT SANTA MARIA DELLA SALUTE, A BAROQUE CHURCH IN VENICE.

+ ANTONIO VIVALDI +

Antonio Vivaldi was an Italian composer who wrote around 800 works, including many operas and concertos. His set of four violin concertos called *The Four Seasons* remains one of the most popular musical works ever written. Vivaldi was a priest in Venice, and his striking red hair earned him the nickname "the Red Priest." He eventually gave up being a priest to concentrate on his music.

+ AWESOME INSTRUMENT +
VIOLIN

THE VIOLIN HAS FOUR STRINGS AND IS MAINLY PLAYED WITH A BOW. It was originally played only to accompany dancers. In the 1660s, a famous violin maker, Antonio Stradivari, apprenticed at another famous violin maker's workshop. Stradivari went on to produce more than 1,100 extraordinary instruments. Known as Stradivarius violins, some of them are still played today. The last Stradivarius was made in 1737, when Stradivari was 92 years old.

STRADIVARIUS VIOLIN ➤

The world's most expensive instrument is a Stradivarius violin—it sold for $15.9 million in 2011.

 LISTEN UP!
JOHANN PACHELBEL, "CANON IN D MAJOR"

[TUNEFUL Terms]

Baroque composers wrote two types of concertos: a concerto grosso, in which a small group of soloists plays separately from the rest of the orchestra; and a concerto solo, which features a single instrument in front of an orchestra. Composers often wrote difficult music for solo concertos so the star musician could show off his or her skills.

A VIOLINIST PERFORMING A CONCERTO SOLO

He's **Bach**, Baby

NO QUESTION, THE FATHER OF BAROQUE MUSIC WAS THE GERMAN COMPOSER JOHANN SEBASTIAN BACH. He was a skilled organ player and wrote a lot of pieces for the organ. While he's celebrated today, in his day, some people thought his music was old-fashioned. But Bach's genius has even influenced rock and pop music: his *Toccata and Fugue in D Minor* has been covered by rock bands, including Sky and Muse.

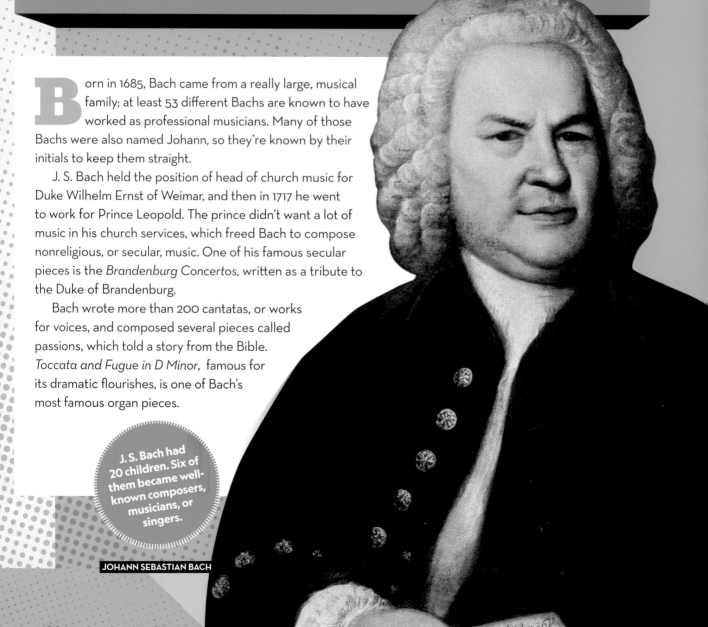

orn in 1685, Bach came from a really large, musical family; at least 53 different Bachs are known to have worked as professional musicians. Many of those Bachs were also named Johann, so they're known by their initials to keep them straight.

J. S. Bach held the position of head of church music for Duke Wilhelm Ernst of Weimar, and then in 1717 he went to work for Prince Leopold. The prince didn't want a lot of music in his church services, which freed Bach to compose nonreligious, or secular, music. One of his famous secular pieces is the *Brandenburg Concertos,* written as a tribute to the Duke of Brandenburg.

Bach wrote more than 200 cantatas, or works for voices, and composed several pieces called passions, which told a story from the Bible. *Toccata and Fugue in D Minor,* famous for its dramatic flourishes, is one of Bach's most famous organ pieces.

J. S. Bach had 20 children. Six of them became well-known composers, musicians, or singers.

JOHANN SEBASTIAN BACH

★

+ MUSICAL MASTER +

GEORG PHILIPP
+ **TELEMANN** +

German composer Georg Philipp Telemann wrote his first opera when he was just 12 years old, but his family wanted him to study law, not music. By chance, young Telemann met the composer George Frideric Handel (see p. 31), who persuaded Telemann to keep at it. He did, and he became famous in Germany, earning far more than his lesser known colleague at the time, J. S. Bach. Telemann wrote more compositions than any other composer of his era.

🔊 LISTEN UP!
J. S. BACH, *THE WELL-TEMPERED CLAVIER*

> The world's largest organ was built in New Jersey, U.S.A., in 1930. It has 33,112 pipes.

+ AWESOME INSTRUMENT +
ORGAN

ORGANS DATE BACK TO THE ANCIENT GREEKS and became popular in churches because they could be played loudly. An organ makes sounds by squeezing air through a set of pipes. An organist chooses which pipe to play by pressing a key on a keyboard or a pedal. Zacharias Hildebrandt and Gottfried Silbermann, two Baroque-era craftsmen, built organs with particularly rich and warm tones. Composers, including Bach and Telemann, always wanted to work where they had access to the best organs.

A PIPE ORGAN HAS 61 KEYS AND SEVERAL SETS OF PIPES, KNOWN AS RANKS.

Hark! A Harpsichord!

THE HARPSICHORD LOOKS A LOT LIKE A PIANO, but its strings are plucked instead of hit. Harpsichords are especially good for playing pieces with two or more melodies. These complex tunes were popular during the Baroque era, making the harpsichord a key instrument of the time. Today, the harpsichord isn't used all that much, but its distinct metallic sound has turned up in songs by The Beatles and in the old classic television show *The Addams Family*.

The harpsichord makes a rich, clear sound that cannot be made louder or softer. Baroque musicians played it alongside singers and to perform solos. Many pieces composed for several instruments had a bass line, which the harpsichord played. Musicians also used the instrument to fill in gaps between other parts and to keep the music moving. Harpsichords were found in many homes, so it made sense that printed music for keyboard instruments was the first type available for purchase.

All the great Baroque composers wrote music for the harpsichord, including Bach, Handel, and Domenico Scarlatti. Scarlatti eventually moved to Spain and wrote keyboard sonatas based on Spanish folk music, creating a type of music that is sometimes known as Iberian Baroque.

DOMENICO SCARLATTI

You can find a recording online of the world's oldest playable harpsichord, which was built around 1530.

THE HARPSICHORD'S STRINGS ARE PLUCKED BY PLECTRUMS KNOWN AS QUILLS.

+ GEORGE FRIDERIC HANDEL +

The German composer George Frideric Handel started out as a harpsichord player. While living in Italy, he wrote many operas. Then, in 1710, he went to work for a German prince who became King George I of England. Handel moved to London, where he spent the rest of his life composing suites, concertos, and music for royal celebrations. One of his most famous pieces is *Water Music*, written for concerts on the Thames River.

[TUNEFUL **Terms**]

Handel wrote a collection of suites in London. A suite opens with a prelude, then a serious movement (a section of music with its own beginning and end) called an *allemande*, followed by a dance called a *courante*, and finally a dance called a *sarabande*. Although suites are for dances, people did not always dance to the music in Handel's time.

TWO DANCERS PERFORM A SARABANDE.

Handel got into a duel with another composer after they argued over the seating in an orchestra pit.

LISTEN UP!

HANDEL, SUITE NO. 5 IN E MAJOR, "THE HARMONIOUS BLACKSMITH"

[BEHIND **the Notes**]

During this time, composers from Europe traveled to the Americas to compose music for churches. The indigenous people they came across, including the Aztec, Maya, and Inca, all had their own rich musical traditions. The traveling composers were inspired by these sounds and rhythms, and they incorporated them into their own pieces. This blend of indigenous and European music became known as New World Baroque music.

A NATIVE PERUVIAN MUSICIAN PLAYING A HUANCAR DRUM AND PANPIPES CALLED SIKU

SO MANY MAGNIFICENT MUSICIANS HAVE NOT YET GOTTEN THEIR DUE IN MUSIC HISTORY. Here are some lesser known and visionary composers from all over the globe during this early time.

BIEIRIS DE ROMANS

12th or 13th century

Bieiris was a composer from France in the 12th or 13th century. She was a trobairitz, or a female troubadour, hailing from southeastern Europe (see p. 15). She was among the first known Western women to write nonreligious music. Although we don't know much about her, Bieiris (thought to be an early version of the name Beatrice) was educated and probably from a noble family. She might have sung at the court of one of the rulers of Occitania. She left behind one love song (or canso) called Na Maria, or "Lady Maria."

AN ILLUSTRATION OF A TROBAIRITZ FROM A MEDIEVAL COLLECTION OF LYRICS, POEMS, AND SONGS

HILDEGARD OF BINGEN

1098–1179

At a time when women were often expected not to be heard, Hildegard of Bingen became one of the most respected voices in all of medieval Europe. A nun who had powerful visions of heavenly fire, Hildegard never learned to write, so she dictated many books. She was so well respected that the Pope sought her advice. She is best known for her religious music, which were beautiful chants with a single melody. Composers today are still influenced by her otherworldly melodies.

MIAN TANSEN

ca. 1500–ca. 1589

Mian ("Master") Tansen was a medieval Indian composer with a legendary life. He is reputed to have created many classics of Hindu music. According to legend, as a boy he could perfectly imitate animals, such as big cats. Another legend holds that he was unable to hear or speak until a saint blew in his mouth and ears. Tansen is known to have gone to the palace of the Mughal emperor Akbar, where he became the greatest Hindu musician ever. It was said that his songs could start fires, and that his wife saved him from burning by singing a rain song.

GASPAR FERNANDES

1566–1629

Before the arrival of Columbus, indigenous peoples in the Americas didn't traditionally write down their music. But thanks to groundbreaking musicians such as the Portuguese-Mexican composer Gaspar Fernandes, we have pieces that link back to the Aztec. As well as composing religious songs in Latin, he wrote songs in multiple native languages. He created a kind of Christmas carol called "Xicochi" (which means "sleep" in Nahuatl, the language of the indigenous peoples of Mexico), and also wrote pieces in the languages of the Africans who were brought to Mexico as slaves.

JEAN-BAPTISTE LULLY

1632–1687

The greatest Baroque composer in France was born and trained in Italy, but he worked for Louis XIV of France. He started off as a dancer, then he became a composer. Thanks to his friendship with the king, he was made a noble and became fantastically rich. Lully was the only person in France allowed to write operas. While conducting a performance of his *Te Deum*, he banged his toe with the staff he used to keep time. The wound became infected and Lully later died.

GUSTAVO DUDAMEL CONDUCTS THE VIENNA PHILHARMONIC,
ONE OF THE FINEST ORCHESTRAS IN THE WORLD.

Isn't It
Romantic...

The 18th and 19th centuries would see astounding developments in Western music, from an emphasis on melody and emotion to the rise of some great musical geniuses (we're looking at you, Mozart and Beethoven). Not to mention the creation of many of the most popular pieces of classical music. Classical and Romantic music played a part in the cultural and social revolutions of the period, while traditional folk music started evolving into popular music. As opera blossomed in Europe, Beijing opera grew in popularity in China, coming to play an important role in the country's cultural life.

Orchestrating
Orchestras

BY THE MID-1700s, ORCHESTRAS, or large groups of musicians playing together, were becoming so popular across Europe that many classical composers started writing music specifically for them instead of just for patrons. This led to an exciting new form of orchestral music: the symphony. Some symphonies are so complex and ambitious that an orchestra might need more than 90 musicians to pull them off. When so many different instruments play together perfectly, there's no denying how powerful classical music can be.

"Orchestra" is an ancient Greek word that refers to the area in front of a stage. That's where musicians sat when the Greeks put on their plays, and eventually the word came to mean "the place where the musicians sit." By the 18th century, the term was used to refer to a group of musicians. The number of musicians, and even the types of instruments they played, would change a lot over time.

The classical orchestra as we know it today took shape in central Europe, primarily in the city of Vienna, Austria. Three superstar composers were writing music for the orchestra during the 19th century: Joseph Haydn, Wolfgang Amadeus Mozart, and Ludwig van Beethoven.

The earliest orchestras were pretty small, mostly made up of string instruments. The best violinist in the group usually directed the other musicians, because orchestras didn't have conductors at the time. As orchestras got bigger, more instruments joined in, including bassoons, oboes, flutes, and clarinets. These woodwinds added different sounds to the music. Brass instruments, including horns and trumpets, also played important parts in the orchestra. After a while, the piano joined the party, replacing the harpsichord. And who could forget the booming timpani (kettle drums)?

Composer Johann Fischer wrote a symphony for eight different timpani.

AN ORCHESTRA PERFORMS VIVALDI'S FOUR SEASONS.

+ JOSEPH HAYDN +

Joseph Haydn started out singing as a choirboy in Vienna, Austria, and he later became a teacher and then a court musician in Hungary. Haydn composed many pieces of amazingly original music. Among his most famous compositions are his 107 symphonies, some of which were written during a 1790s trip to London (see "Listen Up!" below). Haydn was buddies with Mozart, and would go on to teach a certain music student by the name of Beethoven.

[TUNEFUL **Terms**]

A sonata is a piece of music written for a keyboard and one other instrument. Classical sonatas have three movements. The first and last movements are played fast, while the middle one is slow. Haydn, Mozart, and Beethoven all wrote superior sonatas, some of which they turned into full-scale symphonies. A classical symphony usually includes four movements: the first is fast, the second is slow, the third is a lively minuet (dance), and the fourth is fast again.

A SONATA FOR PIANO AND FLUTE

🔊 LISTEN UP!
JOSEPH HAYDN, SYMPHONIES 93–104:
THE LONDON SYMPHONIES
INCLUDING NO. 94, *THE SURPRISE*
NO. 100, *THE MILITARY* NO. 101, *THE CLOCK*

The biggest clarinet, the contrabass, is 9 feet (2.7 m) long.

CLARINET ➤

+ AWESOME INSTRUMENT +
WOODWIND

SOME OF THE WORLD'S OLDEST INSTRUMENTS ARE WOODWINDS. Originally made of wood (although now they're mostly metal), musicians blow into woodwind instruments to play them. A recorder makes a sound when someone blows into one end of it. A flute plays a note when air is blown across the hole in its mouthpiece. Clarinets, saxophones, and oboes all rely on reeds, or thin pieces of cane, that fit into the mouthpiece and vibrate when air is blown into them.

Maximum **Mozart**

ONE DAY IN 1756, IN SALZBURG, AUSTRIA, A BABY BOY WHO WOULD CHANGE THE HISTORY OF MUSIC WAS BORN. His parents named him Wolfgang Amadeus Mozart. He turned out to be a child prodigy, someone who shows true talent for a particular skill at a young age, and he was composing music by the age of five. Although he only lived to be 35, Mozart gave the world a huge amount of music, from symphonies to operas.

Not surprisingly, Mozart came from a musical family. His father, Leopold, was a composer and his sister, Maria Anna, was talented, too. Mozart began learning to play the piano when he was three. By the time he was seven, he was setting off on a three-year tour of Europe, giving concerts with his father and sister.

When he was in his twenties, Mozart was already composing music so outstanding that much of it is still played today. He wrote almost every type of music, including pieces for the piano alone and concertos, which often feature demanding piano solos.

Mozart later moved to Vienna, where audiences went crazy for his symphonies, concertos, and chamber pieces. But when a war between Austria and Turkey broke out in 1788, far fewer concerts were staged. So, Mozart headed to Germany in hopes of continuing his success. But he proved to be less popular there. Back he went to Vienna, where he had a hit with his opera *The Magic Flute*. Just when things were looking up for Mozart, tragedy struck. He died after a sudden illness in 1791, leaving his last work, *Requiem in D Minor*, unfinished.

The Magic Flute includes some of the highest notes possible to sing.

THE LOS ANGELES OPERA PERFORMS *THE MAGIC FLUTE.*

LISTEN UP!
WOLFGANG AMADEUS MOZART,
EINE KLEINE NACHTMUSIK

WOLFGANG AMADEUS MOZART

+ AWESOME INSTRUMENT +
PIANO

MOZART WAS ONE OF THE FIRST GREAT COMPOSERS TO EMBRACE THE PIANO. The piano he would have played was smaller and quieter than modern grand pianos, but they were otherwise similar. When a pianist presses one of the 88 keys, a felt-covered hammer inside the piano strikes a specific string. The string vibrates against a soundboard, which amplifies the sound. Three pedals can be used to alter the piano's sound.

THE COLOR OF THE KEYS ON 18TH-CENTURY PIANOS (RIGHT) WERE SOMETIMES THE REVERSE OF TODAY'S PIANOS.

Most pianos have between 220 and 230 strings made of steel.

VIENNA'S FINE NEW MARKET IN 1790—BOTH MOZART AND HAYDN LIVED NEARBY.

[BEHIND **the Notes**]

It would have been hard to visit late-18th-century Vienna and avoid hearing music. The city overflowed with it. Many people played at least one instrument, and it wasn't uncommon for wealthier music lovers to hire composers to write original pieces for them to play privately at home. Public concerts where pianist-composers, such as Mozart, could showcase their work happened frequently, and operas were regularly staged. No wonder so many great classical composers worked there.

Chamber Music

AT THE SAME TIME ENORMOUS ORCHESTRAS WERE PLAYING TO LARGE AUDIENCES, smaller groups—three to five musicians max—that played chamber music were also becoming popular. These musicians were paid to entertain nobles in the small rooms—or chambers—of their palaces. That's where the term "chamber music" came from. Traditional folk music, handed down through the generations, was also popular. And, thanks largely to Franz Schubert, these traditional tunes also began to pop up in chamber music.

HAYDN (IN THE LIGHT BLUE JACKET) LEADS A STRING QUARTET IN VIENNA.

At first, chamber music performances featured just a few musicians playing privately. However, by the late 1700s, the trend had become so big that the pieces were often performed in public, too.

Today, chamber music is usually played by an ensemble, or small group, with one musician playing each part. An ensemble can be made up of a trio (three musicians), a quintet (five musicians), or most commonly, a quartet (four musicians). Quartets usually have four string instruments (two violins, a viola, and a cello) and are often called string quartets.

Both Haydn and Mozart loved composing for string quartets—sometimes they even played together in Vienna as part of a quartet. During the Romantic era (see pp. 44-45), composers began to incorporate folk music into their chamber pieces. The voice also started being used in chamber music around this time. Composer Franz Schubert became well known for his lieder (German for "songs"), especially "Trout Quintet," which he wrote for four string instruments and a piano.

FRANZ SCHUBERT PLAYS THE PIANO AT THE HOME OF ONE OF HIS FRIENDS.

+ FRANZ SCHUBERT +

Franz Peter Schubert was a Viennese composer who started out by setting poetry to music. Eventually, he went on to write more than 600 lieder, including collections of songs called song cycles, such as *Winterreise* (Winter Journey). Schubert also wrote many other chamber pieces and sonatas. All of his pieces were composed in only a few short years, because he was often ill, and he died in 1828 at only 31 years old.

> **Some say when Schubert first met Beethoven, he was so nervous he ran away.**

[BEHIND the Notes]

While Schubert was not well known during his lifetime—many of his works were never even performed until after his death—today he is considered one of the great Viennese composers, right alongside Mozart and Beethoven. A village in Austria even holds a festival called the Schubertiade every year, which celebrates his life and work. The Schubertiade allows for about 35,000 fans to get their Schubert fix as well as lets them hear pieces by many other composers.

THE VILLAGE OF SCHWARZENBERG HOSTS THE SCHUBERTIADE EACH YEAR.

 **LISTEN UP!**
FRANZ SCHUBERT, "THE TROUT QUINTET"

> **Watch the musical *Fiddler on the Roof* to hear some klezmer tunes.**

[TUNEFUL Terms]

String quartets play more than just chamber music. In the early 1800s, they might also have played klezmer music. "Klezmer" comes from a Yiddish word for "musician." Jewish people in Eastern Europe have played klezmer since medieval times. The music blends religious music with the music of the Romani people. Later, the clarinet, trumpet, trombone, and tuba joined the klezmer sound. In the early 20th century, when some musicians headed to North America, they took their music with them. Klezmer's popularity grew and spread around the world.

KLEZMER MUSICIANS

The Best of Beethoven

EVEN IF YOU DON'T KNOW IT, CHANCES ARE YOU'VE HEARD AT LEAST SOME OF BEETHOVEN'S MUSIC. Ludwig van Beethoven is a towering figure in classical music. He wrote exciting works for orchestras as well as memorable melodies and shorter pieces that appeal to the youngest of music lovers. Beethoven came along after Haydn and Mozart, and he helped create a new style of music. Full of passion, soul, and imagination, Romantic music is about expressing feelings through music, which some people found shocking at the time.

Today, many people consider Beethoven to have been the greatest classical music composer of all time. His symphonies changed the way people thought about classical music. He was born in Germany but lived in Vienna, Austria, for most of his life. He met Mozart as a young man and also studied with Haydn. Beethoven first became known as a skillful pianist in the 1790s, but he was soon celebrated for the original and daring music he composed. He wrote mainly for himself at a time when other composers were writing for wealthy patrons. His pieces had beautiful, expressive melodies that ushered in the Romantic era.

Beethoven began to lose his hearing in 1798 and was completely deaf by 1819. He communicated with people in writing. Yet he never stopped composing and created some of the greatest symphonies and sonatas ever. He never married, but he was in love with a mystery woman he called his "Immortal Beloved." When he died, he was nationally mourned in Austria. Today, Beethoven's music is performed more than any other classical composer's, including his famous piano piece "Für Elise" and his Symphony No. 5 in C Minor.

Beethoven published his first piece of music at the age of 12.

LUDWIG VAN BEETHOVEN

A recording of a song played on the guqin was sent into space by NASA.

+ MUSICAL MASTER +

+ URAGAMI GYOKUDO +

When Beethoven was creating groundbreaking works in the early 19th century, music, painting, and poetry were all considered to be connected. And similar ideas were taking hold in Japan at around the same time. Artists called *bunjin* wrote and played music, painted, and made beautiful writing called calligraphy. One bunjin, Uragami Gyokudo, was a samurai (warrior) who retired to practice his art. Today, he is famous for his paintings, but in his lifetime he was best known for playing the *guqin*, a guitarlike instrument.

[BEHIND the Notes]

Beethoven's Symphony No. 9, which he composed in 1824, finishes with a chorus singing the "Ode to Joy." It's considered one of the most triumphant pieces of classical music written. But what does it mean? Experts have different ideas. One theory says that the symphony is a kind of coded revolutionary message about brotherhood between all people. During a time when some powerful rulers were taking freedoms away from the masses, it would have been a gutsy statement.

A LARGE CHOIR SINGS "ODE TO JOY," THE FINALE OF SYMPHONY NO. 9.

SLIDE TROMBONE ▶

+ AWESOME INSTRUMENT +
BRASS

BRASS INSTRUMENTS ARE MADE OUT OF BRASS OR OTHER METAL AND HAVE METAL MOUTHPIECES. When Beethoven started composing music, brass instruments, such as horns, could play only a few notes. But in about 1815, brass instrument makers began adding valves that allowed for musicians to play many more notes. The change was a hit. Another way to add to a brass instrument's range is by adjusting the length of its tube, such as with the slide of a trombone.

🔊 **LISTEN UP!**
BEETHOVEN, "MOONLIGHT SONATA"

Isn't It Romantic?

THROUGHOUT MUCH OF THE 19TH CENTURY, the Romantic movement influenced art and literature around the world. Romanticism generally focused on imagination and emotion, but it meant different things in different places. In France, Italy, and especially German-speaking areas, Romanticism had a huge impact on music. Suddenly, composers were free to create works that expressed who they were instead of writing music that their patrons wanted from them. Musicians took this newfound freedom and ran with it.

Emotions became more important than ever before with Romantic music. Composers tried to express moods, feelings, and stories in their pieces. They drew inspiration from just about anything—nature, faraway places, legends, even the moonlight. Romantic composers often borrowed ideas from poems, plays, fairy tales, and paintings. They also turned to the culture and traditions of ordinary people, weaving folk dances, local music, and national legends into their pieces.

Some of the music composed by Haydn and Mozart was considered Romantic, but Beethoven was the first to make the style famous. Beethoven loved nature and wrote a symphony named the *Pastoral*, which uses music to tell a story the audience can follow. One of his most famous symphonies, the *Eroica* (Latin for "heroic"), took Romanticism to a new level, sounding grander and more dramatic than most music at the time. The symphony celebrates the hero—someone who is brave and unafraid to follow his own path.

Beethoven's *Pastoral* symphony was originally called *Recollections of Country Life.*

"LIGHT IN THE FOREST," PAINTED IN A ROMANTIC STYLE BY THE GERMAN-AMERICAN ARTIST ALBERT BIERSTADT

Symphonie Fantastique is often described as a self-portrait of Berlioz's own emotions.

[TUNEFUL Terms]

Program music describes a story, event, or scene. The first great example was Beethoven's Symphony No. 6 in F major, *Pastoral*. Beethoven gave each movement a title, such as "Joyous gathering of the country folk" or "Thunderstorm," to help listeners imagine the scene. Berlioz's *Symphonie Fantastique* also titles each movement, building up a story about tortured love and a mysterious journey. Ah, the romance.

THE FINAL MOVEMENT OF *SYMPHONIE FANTASTIQUE* TAKES PLACE AT A GATHERING OF WITCHES AND DEMONS.

+ MUSICAL MASTERS +

+ LOUIS-HECTOR BERLIOZ +

Louis-Hector Berlioz is considered the most important French Romantic composer. In 1830, he wrote his first major work, the *Symphonie Fantastique*, about his love for an actress he had seen in a play. Two years later, he married her. His music, typical of the Romantic period, is full of passion. While Berlioz is celebrated today, he was better known as a conductor than as a composer in his lifetime.

[BEHIND the Notes]

Writing and music inspired and informed each other during the Romantic era, with many poems being written about music and much music inspired by poetry. Schubert composed his first song using a poem by the German poet Goethe. Felix Mendelssohn composed music based on Shakespeare's *A Midsummer Night's Dream*. Another Shakespeare play, *Romeo and Juliet*—maybe you've heard of it?—inspired many musical pieces, from Berlioz and others. How could they not be moved by the tragic love story?

A PERFORMANCE OF THE BALLET *ROMEO AND JULIET*

LISTEN UP!

HECTOR BERLIOZ, *SYMPHONIE FANTASTIQUE*

Totally **Talented**

THE ROMANTICS OFTEN CREATED MUSICAL PIECES THAT CELEBRATED THE HERO CHARACTER, who was typically a lonely guy or girl who rebelled against authority and wasn't afraid to express his or her feelings, no matter the cost. Musicians themselves also came to be viewed as heroes—although today we'd call them celebrities. The most talented among them, known as virtuosi, drew huge audiences and often sold out their performances. Virtuosi were kind of like today's pop stars.

A virtuoso is someone who is especially talented in art, music, singing, or playing an instrument. Virtuosi were the big-name celebrities of the Romantic era. They were a major crowd draw, people wrote about them, and they definitely had dedicated fans. It was common practice to claim a concert would be a musician's last to be sure of big audiences. Virtuoso violinist Niccolò Paganini never disappointed his followers and provided plenty for them to gossip about. Some people believed he had practiced his playing while he was in prison. Another story claimed that he played so well because he'd sold his soul to the devil.

Just as we might follow celebrities on social media today, people during the Romantic era were fascinated by virtuosi appearances. Famous pianist Franz Liszt was often portrayed with unnaturally long, slender fingers. A newspaper report about Liszt declared him "The All-Conquering Pianist," and described a concert where a crowd of women surrounded him to watch his fingers as he played. There were female virtuosi too, including Wilma Neruda from what is now known as the Czech Republic, who became one of the most celebrated violin virtuosi of her time.

WILMA NERUDA

Paganini was forced to publish his mother's letters to prove he was human.

NICCOLÒ PAGANINI

FRANZ LISZT

+ MUSICAL MASTERS +

+ PAGANINI AND LISZT +

Niccolò Paganini, the violin virtuoso, composed pieces that showed off his incredible skills. He was the first violinist to play by plucking the violin strings with his left hand (which holds the violin) instead of the right hand. Paganini was a true showman, and his amazing performances inspired many younger musicians, including the Hungarian pianist and composer Ferenc (Franz) Liszt. Liszt went on to study music in Vienna and tour across Europe. He was successful and donated generously to charities, schools, and hospitals.

🔊 LISTEN UP!
FRÉDÉRIC CHOPIN,
WALTZ IN D FLAT MAJOR, OP. 64, NO. 1, THE "MINUTE WALTZ"

Liszt was such an intense piano player that the piano strings used to break.

CHOPIN PLAYING THE PIANO AT A PARTY HOSTED BY PRINCE ANTONI RADZIWILL

+ MUSICAL MASTER +

+ FRÉDÉRIC CHOPIN +

Frédéric Chopin was considered a piano prodigy. Born in Poland, as a boy he played privately for wealthy people. Later, he moved to Paris, a city that has a long history of attracting artists, musicians, and writers, to be a concert performer. Chopin eventually stopped giving public performances, preferring to play at trendy parties instead. He composed music for the piano and some chamber music, basing some of his pieces on the Polish folk music he'd heard as a child.

[BEHIND the Notes]

Back in Beethoven's day, wealthy patrons paid musicians to compose and perform for them and their guests privately. But a lot of people—not just the wealthy—wanted to attend concerts. The building of the first concert halls began at the end of the 18th century. After 1810, music societies started to put on concert series, and musicians were paid to play in symphony orchestras. One of these, the New York Philharmonic, began in 1842 and still performs today.

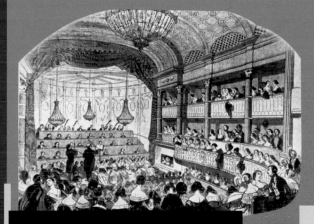

THE SALLE DU CONSERVATOIRE CONCERT HALL IN PARIS

The Outstanding **Orchestra**

AN ORCHESTRA IS A LARGE GROUP OF MUSICIANS PLAYING TOGETHER. Orchestras come in all different sizes, so it is hard to say exactly what is the difference between a band and an orchestra. The orchestra in this photo is a symphony orchestra, which is the largest kind with up to 100 or more musicians. A chamber orchestra is medium size, with around 50 people, while a string orchestra usually has around eight musicians, all playing string instruments.

BACK-ROW BEATS Percussion instruments, such as the bass drum, cymbal, and bells, sit in the back row on the left.

ROOM TO PLAY Large instruments, such as the piano or harp, sit on the left behind the violins.

VIOLIN SECTIONS The violins are in the first few rows to the far left of the conductor—there might be two violin sections, if the orchestra is big enough.

STRING SECTION The front rows are usually for the string instruments.

SEMICIRCLES So that all the musicians are facing the conductor, an orchestra is usually arranged in a semicircle.

WOODWIND Flutes, piccolos, bassoons, and other woodwind instruments sit in two rows behind the strings in the center.

ON YOUR FEET Musicians who need to stand to play their instruments go in the back row, so they don't block the view of those in front.

BACK-ROW BRASS Tubas, trumpets, trombones, and other brass instruments sit in the back rows, mostly to the right of the conductor.

DOUBLING UP To make sure each section can be heard, most instruments in the orchestra are doubled (there are two of them), tripled (three of them), or more.

CONDUCTOR This is the person who stands in front of the orchestra and tells them what to do. Conductors set the speed and rhythm for the orchestra, and they help all the different musicians play together as one.

BIG STRINGS Larger string instruments, such as the violas and cellos, are in the first few rows to the right of the conductor, with the big double basses just behind them.

Symphonic Shifts

BEETHOVEN MADE THE SYMPHONY THE MOST IMPORTANT form of classical music writing. Thousands of symphonies were written by composers during the second half of the 18th century—no one could get enough of them. But between 1825 and 1875, the numbers dropped dramatically. Beethoven was a tough act to follow, and so composers experimented with new ideas and looked to push the symphony in new directions.

Composers began to write pieces with a single movement, called symphonic poems. Symphonies remained popular in Germany and France, where Beethoven's Symphony No. 9 had been a smash hit, but tastes had changed in Italy. The symphony wasn't performed there for years after its debut. The decrease in symphonies might also have been related to Beethoven's dominating talent. Many composers thought that no one could improve on his symphonies, so there was no point in trying.

But composing began to shift again in the late 1800s. An Austrian composer named Anton Bruckner wrote several major symphonies, and Johannes Brahms (see p. 65), a German composer, wrote symphonies that combined tradition and innovation. Brahms greatly admired Beethoven, and even had a statue of him in his studio. He kept the traditional symphony form, but experimented with new techniques.

Then after 1900, Gustav Mahler upped the composing game, writing massive symphonies that he said explored the big questions of life, joy, and grief. He wrote: "Just imagine a work of such magnitude that it mirrors the whole world." No big deal, right? Mahler's symphonies also featured vocal solos and choruses, and he gave them names, such as "The Joyful Knowledge."

ANTON BRUCKNER

A PERFORMANCE OF BEETHOVEN'S SYMPHONY NO. 9

Symphony No. 9 was the first major symphony to include a choir.

+ MUSICAL MASTER +

+ CLARA SCHUMANN +

Clara Wieck was a German child prodigy who became a piano virtuoso. She began performing at just nine years old. When she was only 15, she fell in love with the pianist and composer Robert Schumann, who was one of her father's students. They married against her father's wishes, but Clara Schumann went on to help make her husband's work famous by performing his pieces on stage. She did the same for her buddy Brahms. Clara was a composer, too, and became an influential teacher in her own right.

[TUNEFUL Terms]

A symphonic poem is a piece of music written for an orchestra that usually has just one movement. Closely related to program music (see p. 45), symphonic poems tell stories or describe pictures through music. They're often based on or inspired by specific poems or paintings. The Hungarian composer Franz Liszt invented the symphonic poem (he wrote 13 of them), and this type of music became popular in the second half of the 19th century.

LISZT'S SYMPHONIC POEM *THE BATTLE OF THE HUNS* WAS INSPIRED BY THIS DRAMATIC PAINTING.

🔊 LISTEN UP!

BRAHMS,
FOURTH MOVEMENT OF SYMPHONY NO. 1 IN C MINOR

+ MUSICAL MASTER +

+ GUSTAV MAHLER +

Mahler said, "A symphony should be like the world: it must embrace everything."

Gustav Mahler was an Austrian conductor and composer who had been taught by the composer Anton Bruckner. Later, he traveled around Europe conducting operas and setting new standards for complexity and ambition in symphonies. His eighth symphony, first performed in 1910, earned the nickname "the Symphony of a Thousand," because it requires a huge number of musicians and performers. No fewer than five choirs took part in a recent performance of it in London's Albert Hall.

The Wonder Women of
Classical Music

WOMEN AREN'T OFTEN CELEBRATED in traditional histories of classical music. Most books rarely mention any female composers. Even today, few female composers are recognized. But that doesn't mean they didn't exist. Who were some of the women composers of the past, and why aren't they as famous as the men? It's time to tell the inspiring tales of these talented women, such as Caccini, Strozzi, and Beach.

For a long time, most people believed not only that women should not write music, but that they weren't capable of doing it. Women faced enormous barriers, which often prevented them from even trying to compose. They weren't allowed to study music at a high level, and they were rarely allowed to perform outside their home. And it was nearly impossible for women to publish music if they did write a piece.

Despite all of this, some women made their dreams of composing happen, and some of their achievements were significant. The Italian Francesca Caccini was the first woman to write an opera. Another Italian, Barbara Strozzi, was a singer and composer in the 17th century who wrote more published music than any man of her era, and at a time when women usually had to publish under a man's name. The French musician Louise Farrenc, born in the early 19th century, became a virtuoso pianist in Paris and was one of the first female music professors in all of Europe. Amy Beach was an American composer and pianist who played an important role in the Second New England School (see p. 56).

BARBARA STROZZI

LOUISE FARRENC

52

[BEHIND the Notes]

It's no wonder that during the golden age of classical music, there wasn't a known female Mozart or Beethoven. Back in the 18th and 19th centuries, many people believed that women's brains weren't wired for musical genius. But genius does not come from nowhere; it's nurtured by society and culture, and it requires opportunity. In the past, women's access to education, and in particular music education, was limited. Very few talented women, who were probably also wealthy, were able to succeed.

Clara Schumann was one of the first pianists to perform from memory.

🔊 LISTEN UP!
AMY BEACH, "HERMIT THRUSH AT MORN"

★ · MUSICAL MASTER ·

+ AMY BEACH +

Born in 1867, Amy Beach was a musical child prodigy and pianist, and she went on to become the first successful female composer in the United States. Beach was the first American woman to write a symphony, the popular *Gaelic Symphony*. She was also a performer, but after she married she limited her appearances to only once a year. After her husband died, she decided to build her reputation and toured Europe. Beach wrote mainly in the Romantic style, but she also experimented with folk music.

Amy Beach's first works were written to accompany poems she liked.

[BEHIND the Notes]

Middle class women of the 19th century were expected to have "accomplishments," such as singing or playing an instrument, but these were seen as hobbies rather than career opportunities. Fanny Mendelssohn, the sister of the famous German composer Felix Mendelssohn, had a musical talent to equal her brother's. She wrote nearly 500 pieces of music, but her gender meant she could never build a career as a composer. Recognizing her exceptional talent, Felix even published some of Fanny's works under his own name.

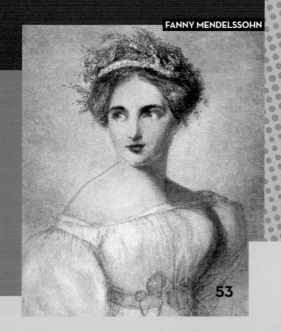
FANNY MENDELSSOHN

Notes of Pride

THE ROMANTIC ERA WAS A PERIOD OF GREAT POLITICAL UPHEAVAL. The Napoleonic Wars created turmoil between almost all of the major countries in Europe, leading to a decade-long state of unrest. By the end of it all, people were left wondering if countries shouldn't be part of larger empires after all. The result was a great feeling of patriotism, or national pride for people in individual countries, which ushered in a musical era known as nationalism. Nationalist composers tried to write music that embraced what was unique about their countries and stirred people's imaginations.

REVOLUTIONS BROKE OUT IN MANY COUNTRIES ACROSS EUROPE IN 1848.

54

Nationalism in music came from the idea that countries had their own identities—and that they should rule themselves. Romantic composers felt able to express their feelings about what was going on politically. The concept that countries shouldn't be part of larger empires was new, and music became an important part of that. Many composers wanted to break with the German influence that had shaped other European music. So they began creating new music styles inspired by the folk tunes and dances of their own countries.

The Austrian composer Haydn was one of the first to use folk songs in his pieces. Chopin was inspired by a Polish dance called the mazurka. Liszt wrote a whopping 19 piano pieces based on Hungarian folk themes. This was a time of revolution in Europe and nationalist feelings encouraged the trend in music. Soon many nations, from Russia to Bohemia, Norway, and Finland, had nationalist music. The trend grew outside of the West, too. In India, Rabindranath Tagore was an important nationalist composer.

FRÉDÉRIC CHOPIN

[BEHIND the Notes]

Ballet grew out of the French court dances of the 17th and 18th centuries. By the 19th century, ballet dancers began to move their bodies more freely (wearing fewer clothes helped), and ballet became especially popular in France when it was performed as part of an opera. The passion for ballet spread from France to Russia, where Tchaikovsky would eventually compose mesmerizing music for Russian ballet dancers to dance to. *The Nutcracker* remains one of the most popular pieces of music ever written.

BALLET DANCERS PERFORM *THE NUTCRACKER.*

LISTEN UP!

EDVARD GRIEG, "IN THE HALL OF THE MOUNTAIN KING," FROM *PEER GYNT*

+ MUSICAL MASTER +

PYOTR ILYICH + TCHAIKOVSKY +

Pyotr Ilyich Tchaikovsky was a Russian composer and conductor who was one of the most popular classical composers. He tried to combine Russian music with classical traditions in his pieces. He led an unhappy life, but today Tchaikovsky is remembered for his beloved ballets, including *The Nutcracker* and *Swan Lake*, his operas, and the nationalist *1812 Overture*, written to mark Russia's victory over Napoleon Bonaparte.

+ MUSICAL MASTERS +

+ SMETANA AND GRIEG +

The composer Bedřich Smetana is regarded as the founder of Czech music. Smetana fought in a nationalist uprising in 1848 and went on to become a national treasure. Today, his most famous work is an opera called *The Bartered Bride*. Edvard Grieg was from Norway and he dedicated his life to writing nationalist music. His most famous music was composed for a play called *Peer Gynt*, written by his fellow countryman and playwright Henrik Ibsen.

Smetana was deaf when he composed his final piece of music.

PEER GYNT MEETS THE TROLL KING IN A HALL DEEP IN THE MOUNTAINS.

Only in America

BECAUSE OF ITS PHYSICAL SEPARATION FROM EUROPE,

the United Stated has developed many different types of music throughout history. Native Americans had their own rich traditions of song and music, as did the people who emigrated there across the centuries. While the various types of music started off separate, slowly they began to influence each other as people traveled more and shared ideas. Today's American music, like the country itself, is a big melting pot, ranging widely in content, style, and form.

Some of the earliest European settlers in North America were the Puritans, a strict religious group. Their music was as conservative as their clothing, and they had a tradition of singing without musical accompaniment. After the Revolutionary War, when some folks had just a little more spare time and money, sales of musical instruments and singing lessons increased. Voice teachers needed something to teach with, which led to the publishing of collections of songs in tunebooks. The creators of these books came to be known as the First New England School (or the native pioneers or Yankee tunesmiths) and they included the composers William Billings, Daniel Read, Timothy Swan, and Supply Belcher.

A Second New England School developed in the late 19th century and included American composers who tried to create distinctly American classical music. Before then, most American classical music was music that had simply come across the ocean with immigrant musicians. Many of the Second School composers, including John Knowles Paine and Edward MacDowell, taught music at universities in and around Boston.

EDWARD MACDOWELL

Supply Belcher was called "The Handell [sic] of Maine" by one newspaper.

TWO DRUMMERS AND A FIFE PLAYER IN ARCHIBALD WILLARD'S FAMOUS PAINTING, "SPIRIT OF '76"

[BEHIND the Notes]

American soldiers often sang ballads and other songs to keep their spirits up during the Revolutionary War. One favorite tune was "Yankee Doodle," which had actually been written by a British commander to mock American soldiers and was set to an old English folk tune. However, the idea backfired. Americans liked the catchy tune and made it their own, even forcing captured British soldiers to dance to it.

DRUMMERS AND FIFE PLAYERS BOOSTED MORALE DURING THE REVOLUTIONARY WAR.

JOHN KNOWLES PAINE

+ MUSICAL MASTERS +

+ PAINE AND BRISTOW +

John Knowles Paine was the first American composer to become famous for writing orchestra music. He also happened to be the first Professor of Music at Harvard University. Paine's works were similar in style to Viennese classical and Romantic pieces. His symphonies and choral works became popular, and they were some of the first pieces by an American composer to be performed in Europe. George Bristow, a violinist, composer, and conductor from New York, aimed to compose music that sounded uniquely American. He was an influential music teacher in public schools.

In 1889, Paine made one of the first musical recordings on wax cylinder.

 **LISTEN UP!**
JOHN DICKINSON, "THE LIBERTY SONG"

[BEHIND the Notes]

Antonín Dvořák was a Czech composer who moved to the United States and wrote nationalist music. In 1892, he became director of the National Conservatory of Music in New York. Dvořák was heavily influenced and inspired by African-American spirituals and Native American music. He believed that the melodies of the spirituals were the real foundation of composition and often wove them into his own pieces, which led him to write his best known work, the *New World Symphony*. After Dvořák's death, "Largo," the symphony's second movement, was turned into "Goin' Home" by his pupil William Arms Fisher.

ANTONÍN DVOŘÁK

57

Strike Up the Band!

DURING THE EARLY 19TH CENTURY, marches made their way off the battlefield and into popular music. Franz Liszt composed pieces based on military marches, and military bands often played for civilian (nonmilitary) audiences. If you've ever attended a Fourth of July concert, you've probably heard music written by one the best known composers of American marches: John Philip Sousa. During his lifetime, Sousa composed a whopping 136 marches, including the well-known "The Stars and Stripes Forever."

STARS AND STRIPES FOREVER SONG.

BY JOHN PHILIP SOUSA

PUBLISHED BY
THE JOHN CHURCH COMPANY
CINCINNATI. NEW YORK. CHICAGO

SHEET MUSIC OF SOUSA'S "THE STARS AND STRIPES FOREVER"

Military bands grew in size about 10 times over in the 19th century, from five musicians in 1800 to 50 or more by 1900. As marches became more popular, composers wrote a lot more of them. Most marches played by military bands were written between 1880 and 1914, the year World War I broke out. During the American Civil War, Union Army band master Patrick Gilmore wrote "When Johnny Comes Marching Home," which was a huge hit when he toured, playing to large audiences.

Sousa proved to be the march master, however, and he composed many marches, including "Semper Fidelis" and "King Cotton." Most of his marches were about four minutes long and were written specifically for the U.S. Marine Band and Sousa's own touring band. His march "The Stars and Stripes Forever" has been recorded by more bands and orchestras than any other march, and "The Washington Post" became a popular dance.

This was truly a golden age of touring bands, and Sousa led one of the best. With as many as 76 musicians, they sometimes played in two towns a day. His band performed more than 15,000 times during 40 years.

AN AMERICAN MARCHING BAND

+ MUSICAL MASTER +

+ JOHN PHILIP SOUSA +

Sousa was born in Washington, D.C., in 1854. By the time he was 13, he'd fallen in love with music and made plans to run away and join a circus band. His dad signed him up as an apprentice in the U.S. Marine Band instead. By 1880, Sousa had become the band's conductor and was also composing marches all the time. Recordings of his pieces sold millions of copies and he conducted thousands of performances.

Sousa's conductor's baton is given to each new leader of the U.S. Marine Band.

LISTEN UP!
JOHANN STRAUSS SR., "RADETZKY MARCH"

+ AWESOME INSTRUMENT +
SOUSAPHONE

THE SOUSAPHONE IS A BASS TUBA with a tube that curves all the way around the player. It's usually used in marching bands and occasionally in jazz bands. Sousa designed the instrument in the early 1890s, and it's named after him. The first models featured wide bells pointing upward and were nicknamed "rain-catchers." Probably not surprisingly, they didn't take off. But when another design shifted the bell so it pointed forward, the instrument became a hit. Sousaphones have been part of the standard marching band lineup ever since.

A brass sousaphone can weigh as much as 50 pounds (22.5 kg)!

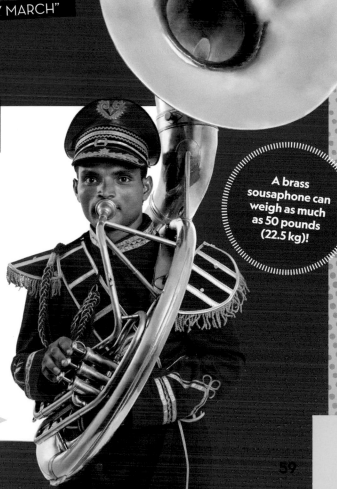

SOUSAPHONE ➤

Opening Up to Opera

DON'T TUNE OUT JUST YET. While opera music might sometimes be hard to understand, it's actually a play, and the actors are singing their parts. It became popular in Europe during the classical music era, especially in Italy. Operas of that time tended to use comedy and included parts that let singers show off their pipes. The Romantic movement ushered in a new type of musical drama, with operas becoming more serious and emotional.

Opera stars in 18th-century France and Italy showed their skills in complicated solos called arias. Mozart made an effort to get instruments and voices working together in the operas he composed, and that led to a new era in opera. By the 19th century, some operas had audiences laughing, especially those by beloved Italian composer Gioachino Rossini. Italians couldn't seem to get enough opera, sometimes going to performances as many as four or five times a week.

At the same time as Rossini's success, a German composer named Carl Maria von Weber was writing Romantic operas about magic and wild places. But it was the German composer Richard Wagner who turned out to have the most influence on Romantic opera. Wagner believed opera should include every kind of art—from using poetry in the lyrics to creating rich paintings and designs for the scenery and costumes—and he used music to heighten the drama of his stories. By the late 19th century, Italian operas had gotten more realistic in style, and composers such as Giacomo Puccini were writing operas with characters who faced tragic lives.

GIOACHINO ROSSINI

Puccini's opera La Bohème was made into a musical called Rent in 1995.

A PERFORMANCE OF PUCCINI'S OPERA LA BOHÈME

+ MUSICAL MASTER +

+ RICHARD WAGNER +

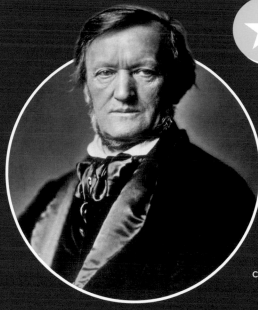

Richard Wagner was a composer, conductor, and writer. He had an eventful life, having fled Germany after being caught up in a revolution, and he then struggled to survive until he won support from King Ludwig of Bavaria. His great life's work was a series of four operas based on Scandinavian legends about heroes, dragons, gods, and a ring of power, called the *Ring Cycle*. He intended all four operas to be performed together, and the first complete performance took place in 1876.

[BEHIND the Notes]

Bayreuth is a small town in Bavaria and this is where Wagner found land and built a home and a theater called the Festspielhaus. It was designed to stage the *Ring Cycle* in 1876. The town has held an opera festival there regularly since 1892, and it has always been run by someone in Wagner's family. The theater holds about 1,800 people and is specially designed to make the singing and the rest of the music sound amazing.

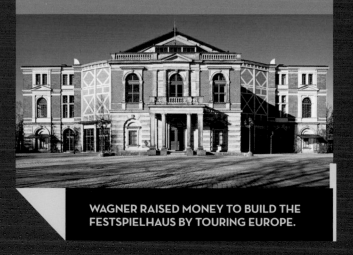

WAGNER RAISED MONEY TO BUILD THE FESTSPIELHAUS BY TOURING EUROPE.

Puccini loved driving fast cars and had a speedboat.

+ MUSICAL MASTER +

GIACOMO + PUCCINI +

Giacomo Puccini was an Italian composer who started writing operas in about 1884. Full of sentimental and emotional music and vivid characters, his operas are some of the best loved of all time, and many are still performed frequently today. His *La Bohème* is the love story of a poet and a seamstress set in Paris. It debuted in Turin, Italy, in 1896 and is probably the most popular opera ever produced. Puccini also wrote the classics *Madame Butterfly* and *Turandot*.

🔊 LISTEN UP!

WAGNER , "RIDE OF THE VALKYRIES," FROM THE BEGINNING OF ACT 3 OF *DIE WALKÜRE*

The Many Moods of
Asian Opera

WHILE OPERA'S POPULARITY GREW IN EUROPE, CHINA EXPERIENCED A BOOM IN ITS OWN RICH OPERA TRADITION, which included a variety of both sounds and kinds of performances. The Beijing jingju, or opera, appeared about 1790. This distinctive type of musical theater was enjoyed throughout the 19th century and had become a national art form by the early 20th century. Meanwhile, in Japan, a traditional style of drama called kabuki, in which actors sing, dance, and play instruments, had been popular for years.

O f the hundreds of styles of Chinese opera, Beijing opera is probably the best known. The spectacle of actors wearing elaborate makeup and singing and practicing martial arts is drama at its finest. Beijing opera features two types of music: lively and upbeat *xipi* and serious, sad *erhuang*. Although it was once viewed as common and not artistic, by 1860, even the emperor's court enjoyed Beijing opera. Empress Cixi, who ruled China for most of the late 19th century, was a huge fan—she even invited performers to live in the palace. Beijing opera only grew in popularity over time and is still performed today.

Meanwhile, Japan's traditional and dramatic kabuki also found success during the 18th century. A kabuki performance features musicians who play and sing offstage. Onstage, dancers and a smaller group of musicians perform together. Kabuki was started by a Japanese woman named Izumo no Okuni back in 1603. It survived and thrived for a solid two centuries before the 19th-century shoguns (warlords) who ruled Japan tried to abolish it. Lucky for us, they didn't succeed.

JAPANESE KABUKI

In Beijing opera, the more elaborate the headdress, the bigger the character.

BEIJING OPERA
PERFORMER

[BEHIND **the Notes**]

WUCHANG DRUMMERS

Unlike Western operas, in which the composer writes the music while a librettist writes the story and words, Beijing opera is created by musicians, actors, singers, and writers who all work together. The singers are accompanied by a small group of musicians divided into two sections—*wenchang* (civilian) featuring lutes and fiddles, and *wuchang* (military) featuring drums and gongs.

LISTEN UP!

CHINA CENTRAL PHILHARMONIC ORCHESTRA & CHOIR, *A GATHERING OF HEROES*

It's not all about singing—each performance also includes martial arts.

+ AWESOME INSTRUMENT +
TRADITIONAL CHINESE INSTRUMENTS

THE *WENCHANG*, OR CIVILIAN, MUSICIAN SECTION of Beijing opera includes several traditional Chinese instruments. The *jinghu* and the *jing erhu* are two-string fiddles played with a bow. The wooden body of the jing erhu is covered with snakeskin at one end. The *yueqin* is a mandolin with two to four strings, and the *suona* is an oboe with a metal bell. The *sanxian* is a lute with three strings and a long neck.

◀ **YUEQIN MANDOLIN**

[TUNEFUL **Terms**]

Another one of the hundreds of Chinese opera styles is Huangmei, which is named after the district in China where it began. Based on *caicha*, or tea-picking tunes that were sung by workers in the tea fields of the region, today Huangmei opera is famous for its sweet tunes and lyrics, graceful movements, and beautiful, historical costumes and sets. The stories are often based on Chinese folktales.

A PERFORMANCE OF THE HUANGMEI OPERA *MARRIAGE OF THE FAIRY PRINCESS*

THE 18TH AND 19TH CENTURIES SAW ART MUSIC BECOME MORE POPULAR, especially styles of music that told stories. All over the world, many musicians and composers contributed their take on music. One young woman in Japan invented a new musical theater that became a little too popular for the government's liking, while an amazing pianist prodigy from Venezuela blew Abraham Lincoln's socks off. In Germany, the best composer since Beethoven is remembered for his beard as well as his music. These are just a few examples of other noteworthy musicians of the time.

IZUMO NO OKUNI

ca. 1571–ca. 1650

This young Japanese woman invented a theater craze so popular that the government banned it. Izumo no Okuni was a priestess at a temple who danced to earn money. She put on exciting shows in which she dressed in men's clothes and acted the men's roles as well as the women's. Her new style of theater was called kabuki, from a Japanese word roughly meaning "breaking the rules." Other women joined in, and people loved seeing kabuki. But the government was worried that these women were having too much fun, so they passed a law stating that only men could act in kabuki. Izumo no Okuni later retired to become a nun.

GIUSEPPE VERDI

1813–1901

One of the greatest opera composers of all time, the Italian Giuseppe Verdi came from a humble background—his father was an innkeeper. His career almost ended just after it had begun, because he was hit by multiple tragedies. His two children died, followed by his wife, and the opera he was writing turned out to be a flop. But Verdi tried again and achieved huge success with an opera called *Nabucco*. He went on to write classic operas including *Rigoletto*, *Aida*, and *Otello*. When he died in 1901, the biggest crowd ever recorded in Italian history came to his funeral.

JOHANNES BRAHMS

1833–1897

Although Brahms wrote impressive music that built on the traditions of the great German composers before him, he found it hard to escape their long shadows. It took Brahms a full 15 years to finish his first symphony—he was worried it would never be good enough. In addition to his music, Brahms is remembered for his famously long beard. He had a very public argument with Richard Wagner; their battle was called the War of the Romantics.

TERESA CARREÑO

1853–1917

When she was six, Teresa Carreño's father, who was a composer, realized that she was already a better musician than him. The Carreño family moved from Venezuela to New York, where the then-nine-year-old Teresa wowed audiences in sold-out concert halls. She even played for Abraham Lincoln at the White House. She later moved to Europe and became a teacher in Germany, earning the nickname Valkyrie of the Piano (after the female warrior spirits in a Viking myth).

MEI LANFANG

1894–1961

For a long time, women were banned from performing in Beijing opera, which meant men took on women's roles. Men who played women were called nandan performers. The most famous nandan ever was Mei Lanfang. He started training when he was just eight years old and learned acting, acrobatics, and singing. Although the work was grueling, Mei became a huge star. He toured the world and brought Beijing opera to international audiences. Two of his nine children followed in his footsteps, with one of his daughters playing male roles (by then times had changed and women were allowed to appear in operas) and one of his sons playing female roles.

CROWDS GATHER FOR A SCREENING OF *CITIZEN KANE* IN 1941. THE SCORE WAS
WRITTEN BY MOVIE MUSIC MAESTRO BERNARD HERRMANN (SEE P. 85).

CHAPTER 3

1900–1950

Thoroughly Modern
Music

In the early years of the 20th century, technology and society were changing fast. This era saw the invention of radio, film, and the recording industry, which led to big changes in music. Musical theater and folk music traditions also became more widely available. Artists explored completely new ways of making music, but not all of it was popular. With challenging rhythms and unusual sounds, some new pieces offended listeners. As easier ways to access music developed, audiences grew, which had a major impact on music all over the world, but especially in the United States.

New Century, New Start

AS A NEW CENTURY DAWNED, like almost everyone else, classical musicians felt a renewed energy, and they used it to try out new ideas. German Romantic music, which had long been the standard, began to feel too old fashioned for modern times. Composers such as Claude Debussy led the way in leaving the rigid rules of traditional classical music in the dust. The turn of the 20th century was a great time for any composer with a rebellious streak.

French composer Claude Debussy had no intention of following in the footsteps of Wagner, whose music he found too dramatic. Inspired by the French painters known as the Impressionists, he wrote pieces that were abstract and lighter in tone. Because of this, his style was also called Impressionist.

Debussy was only one of many composers who began to bend and break the rules of classical music. They experimented with basic fundamentals, such as replacing the standard octave scale of eight notes with a scale that had only five notes, called the pentatonic scale. (Try playing only the black keys on a piano: that's the pentatonic scale.) They explored other new effects, such as dissonance, notes that clash, and syncopation, which uses unexpected rhythms. Composers even rethought how instruments were played, asking musicians to tap the bodies of their violins instead of playing its strings.

The composer Arnold Schoenberg, along with his students Alban Berg and Anton Webern, together came to be known as the Second Viennese School. They used new, daring techniques to create brand-new styles of music. Schoenberg invented Expressionism (another name borrowed from painting), in which dissonance and distorted melodies express feelings and emotions.

CLAUDE DEBUSSY

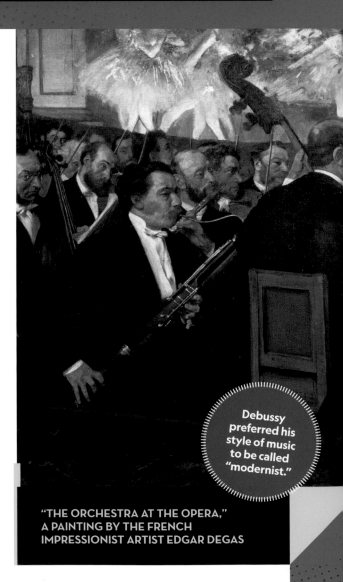

Debussy preferred his style of music to be called "modernist."

"THE ORCHESTRA AT THE OPERA," A PAINTING BY THE FRENCH IMPRESSIONIST ARTIST EDGAR DEGAS

68

★ + MUSICAL MASTER +

+ ARNOLD + SCHOENBERG

Thanks to his innovative ideas about classical music, Arnold Schoenberg was an influential Austrian composer, conductor, and teacher. Schoenberg taught in Vienna, where he had a big impact on the next generation of musicians. People tended to have strong reactions to his challenging pieces, which use dissonance and constantly changing patterns. Maybe that's why he started a private music society in 1918 that banned both critics and applause. When the Nazis came to power in the 1930s, Schoenberg left Europe for North America.

[BEHIND the Notes]

While Schoenberg turned his back on the past, other 20th-century musicians dived into it. Composers such as the Englishman Ralph Vaughan Williams and the Hungarian Béla Bartók collected and took inspiration from traditional folk songs, sometimes copying them or simply capturing their spirit. Their works continued the nationalist movement of the 19th century (see p. 54) and celebrated their homelands.

★ + MUSICAL MASTER +

+ CLAUDE DEBUSSY +

Even as a music student, Achille-Claude Debussy had a reputation for being a rule breaker. In his youth, he met the Hungarian composer Liszt and the Italian opera composer Verdi, and he traveled to Bayreuth to hear Wagner's music, too. But his two biggest influences were his friendships with Impressionist painters and poets and the unique sounds of gamelan percussion instruments from Indonesia (see p. 20). Debussy invented new ways of using scales, harmonies, and chords and tried to create what he called a halo of sound.

The word "gamelan" means "to hammer."

DEBUSSY WAS INSPIRED BY THE SOUNDS OF INDONESIAN GAMELAN ORCHESTRAS LIKE THIS ONE.

 **LISTEN UP!**
CLAUDE DEBUSSY, "L'APRÈS-MIDI D'UN FAUNE"

Riot at the **Ballet**

THE POPULARITY OF BALLET IN RUSSIA played a big role in convincing more composers to take it seriously. It was in Paris, however, that ballet leaped into the modern age. The Ballets Russes dance company gave dramatic performances, presenting the best artists, writers, dancers, and composers all on one stage. The company wanted to shock audiences with unusual choreography and modern music that used harsh rhythms and sounds. They often succeeded: One of their performances caused riots in a theater.

The most important person in Russian ballet at the turn of the 20th century was Marius Petipa, a choreographer credited with inventing classical ballet. A choreographer creates sequences of dance movements. Meanwhile, in the United States, the dancer Isadora Duncan came up with a free, natural style of dancing based on animal movements and the figures painted on ancient Greek vases. Duncan visited Russia, where she inspired a young dancer named Mikhail Fokine. Fokine teamed up with Russian ballet producer Sergei Diaghilev, and together they planned a bold new direction for ballet.

In 1909, they established the Ballets Russes company in Paris. Diaghilev needed new music to match his exciting new company, so he asked young composers to create some. In 1910, Russian composer Igor Stravinsky wrote *The Firebird* for the Ballet Russes, and it was an instant sensation. Three years later, the company staged another Stravinsky ballet, *The Rite of Spring*. The music was harsh, with clashing notes and a driving rhythm, and the dancing was strange and jerky. The performance, which represented rituals from prehistoric times, was so strange that the audience rioted, yelling and throwing things at the stage. Police ended up arresting dozens of people.

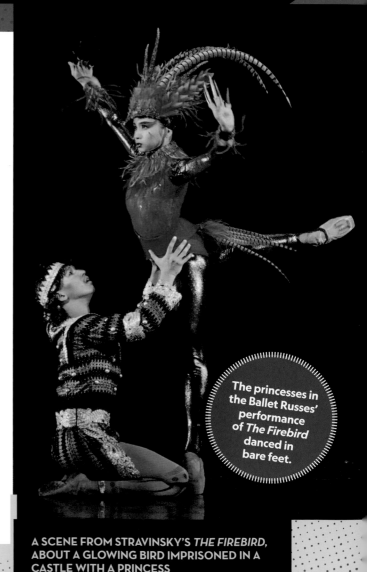

The princesses in the Ballet Russes' performance of *The Firebird* danced in bare feet.

A SCENE FROM STRAVINSKY'S *THE FIREBIRD*, ABOUT A GLOWING BIRD IMPRISONED IN A CASTLE WITH A PRINCESS

+ IGOR STRAVINSKY +

Igor Stravinsky was a Russian pianist, composer, conductor, and writer. He spent a lot of time at the home of the composer Nikolay Rimsky-Korsakov, who later taught him. Stravinsky found fame with the ballets he composed for the Ballets Russes. He became a leading modern composer and never stuck with a single musical style. After Stravinsky left Russia, his music combined Russian folk dances with other styles. Eventually, he even composed in a style inspired by Schoenberg.

A SCENE FROM A 1913 BALLETS RUSSES PRODUCTION OF STRAVINSKY'S *RITE OF SPRING*, PERFORMED IN PARIS, FRANCE

[BEHIND the Notes]

When Sergei Diaghilev created the Ballets Russes, he made sure to work with the most exciting artists and performers of the time. The famous dancer Vaslav Nijinsky danced with the company, and the painter Léon Bakst designed its revolutionary sets and costumes using rich, exotic colors and textures. Famous painters such as Henri Matisse and Pablo Picasso also worked with the Ballet. Diaghilev's company relied on famous musicians including Richard Strauss, Erik Satie, Maurice Ravel, and Sergei Prokofiev.

LISTEN UP!
IGOR STRAVINSKY, "INFERNAL DANCE OF KING KASHCHEI, "FROM *THE FIREBIRD*

+ SERGEI PROKOFIEV +

Sergei Prokofiev was a Russian composer who wrote his first opera at the age of nine. Later, he composed for the Ballets Russes while continuing to write operas. After the Russian Revolution in 1917, he moved to the United States and then to Paris, but he eventually returned to the Soviet Union, where he remained until his death. Today, Prokofiev is most famous for *Peter and the Wolf,* which he wrote to teach young people about the orchestra.

Prokofiev composed *Peter and the Wolf* in less than two weeks.

IN *PETER AND THE WOLF,* EACH CHARACTER IS REPRESENTED BY A PARTICULAR INSTRUMENT.

The Spirit of
Spain and Latin America

SPANISH MUSIC HAS A RICH HISTORY AND INSTANTLY RECOGNIZABLE SOUNDS AND RHYTHMS. Its easy-to-dance-to style has influenced and inspired the music of an enormous region that stretches from the Caribbean and North America all the way down to the tip of South America. The most important instrument in all of Spanish music is undoubtedly the guitar. The iconic sound of quickly plucked strings is a crucial accompaniment to the fiery steps of the flamenco dance.

The fastest ever flamenco dancer performed 1,274 taps in one minute.

The guitar has been a fixture in Spanish music since the Middle Ages, when a type of guitar called the vihuela was a favorite instrument of the powerful Queen Isabella. In the early 19th century, guitar found its way to the heart of Spanish music with the help of Fernando Sor and Dionisio Aguado y García. By the late 19th century, the Romantic nationalist movement reached Spain, with folk songs and dances mainly from the Romani and Moorish traditions becoming popular. It was a French composer named Maurice Ravel, however, who helped spread Spanish influence in classical music.

The culture and music of Latin America is a collection of traditions from an incredibly diverse group, from the indigenous peoples who had always lived there to the people who came from Spain and Portugal and enslaved Africans brought there by force. The combination of music and dances from such varied cultures created many different popular styles. Romantic nationalism found its way to Latin America later than it did in other countries, so Latin composers drew heavily on folk music for inspiration. The Latin influence has even reached as far as southeast Asia, where a form of Vietnamese bolero developed.

FLAMENCO MASTER
PEPE HABICHUELA

FLAMENCO DANCERS EXPRESS THEIR EMOTIONS THROUGH DRAMATIC HAND CLAPS AND HEEL STAMPS.

[TUNEFUL **Terms**]

During the Vietnam War of 1955–75, bolero and other Latin styles of music were popular in South Vietnam. Local musicians matched their musical styles to the rhythms of Latin music, which created a combination of slow, sad love songs called "yellow music." The term might have been a reference to South Vietnam's flag, or it might have been an intentional contrast to the official Communist "red music" of then-North Vietnam. After the two countries joined together again, yellow music became popular everywhere.

FAMOUS VIETNAMESE SINGERS INCLUDE KHÁNH LY (BELOW) AND THANH THÚY.

+ AWESOME INSTRUMENT +
GUITAR

THE GUITAR IS A STRING INSTRUMENT WITH A LONG NECK AND A BODY WITH A WAIST. Related to the lute, it comes from the long-necked string instruments that musicians played in ancient times. The guitar became popular in the 19th century, and was played by famous classical musicians such as Paganini and the virtuoso Andrés Segovia. Later, the guitar came to play an important part in Latin music, and also in the blues, rock, and pop, and it's widely used in many music styles today.

ACOUSTIC GUITAR ➤

[TUNEFUL **Terms**]

Cumbia is a music and dance style that started in the northeastern part of Colombia, near the Caribbean coast, although it's now popular all over Latin America. The name probably comes from cumbe, a rhythmic dance from the Bata region of Equatorial Guinea. Many colonial-era slaves in Colombia came from this region. Cumbia remains big in Colombia, and has even crossed over into other types of Latin and popular music, such as hip-hop.

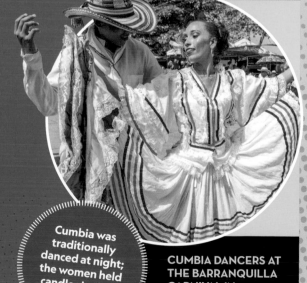

Cumbia was traditionally danced at night; the women held candles in their right hand.

CUMBIA DANCERS AT THE BARRANQUILLA CARNIVAL IN COLOMBIA

🔊 **LISTEN UP!**
ENRIQUE GRANADOS, "SPANISH DANCE NO. 5," PLAYED BY SEGOVIA

73

Anything Goes in America

THE EARLY 20TH CENTURY SAW A NEW GENERATION of composers in the United States creating American classical music. Inspired by folk songs, jazz, African-American music, hymns, and marches, they made music that captured both the country's wide open spaces and the energy of its big cities. War, economic changes, and advances in technology all helped shape their work. It was an exciting time for music, when anything was possible and musical rules were made to be broken.

Advances in communications and technology led to more people enjoying music by listening to sound recordings and buying sheet music. The American composer Charles Ives mixed traditional style with classical music using daring new techniques, such as clashing tones and unexpected rhythms, before they were common in Europe. The military marches and hymns of his childhood inspired him.

Antonín Dvořák, the Czech composer who moved to the United States, encouraged American composers to understand African-American popular music as the true American folk music.

Early jazz would become an important influence on the work of some composers, such as Aaron Copland and George Gershwin. The Great Depression and World War II affected the way musicians worked and how ordinary citizens thought about art music (music written by trained musicians). There was a desire to record the American experience. Roy Harris composed symphonies celebrating American landscapes and the heroic lives of its people. Copland followed suit, producing many popular pieces, including "Appalachian Spring" and "Fanfare for the Common Man."

Copland's music has been used for U.S. presidential inaugurations.

AARON COPLAND

DANCERS PERFORM AARON COPLAND'S BALLET *RODEO.*

+ MUSICAL MASTER +

+ CHARLES IVES +

Charles Ives was an eccentric American composer who was fascinated by clashing sounds, such as when two bands played at the same time. He wrote original and unusual music that was often based on famous pieces or used strange techniques. In his "Concord Sonata," for example, the pianist presses the keys with a piece of wood. Ives died in 1954, leaving a complex, unfinished work called *Universe Symphony*. It was intended to be played by several different orchestras and sung by huge choirs on mountaintops.

The last section of Ives' *Universe Symphony* is called "Heaven."

[BEHIND the Notes]

The Great Depression of the 1930s spread terrible hardship across the United States. To support artists and improve the lives of ordinary people, the government created the Federal Music Project. It taught people to play musical instruments and funded jobs for musicians in orchestras, dance bands, choruses, and even opera companies. Between 1936 and 1940, the FMP staged 250,000 performances for audiences of 159 million people, giving more people than ever before access to different types of music.

A POSTER ADVERTISING THE OPERA CARMEN, SUPPORTED BY THE FMP

+ MUSICAL MASTERS +

AARON COPLAND + AND ROY HARRIS +

Born in New York to Jewish immigrants from Russia, Aaron Copland gained a reputation for writing daring, jazz-influenced music. He wanted modern classical music to be popular, but eventually began composing in a more mainstream style, perhaps influenced by the success of Roy Harris. Harris, a composer from Oklahoma, U.S.A., wrote symphonies that tried to capture the country's unique spirit. His style was strong and bold, often mixing folk music and hymns.

ROY HARRIS

LISTEN UP!
ROY HARRIS, SYMPHONY NO. 3

Gotta Sing, **Gotta Dance!**

IN THE UNITED STATES, THE GREAT AGE OF MUSICALS BEGAN ON BROADWAY IN THE 1920s IN NEW YORK CITY, and it had its golden age in the 1940s and '50s. However, the Broadway musical didn't sit still; it changed with the times and became an international musical sensation. Today, shows such as *Wicked* bring music, dance, and spectacle to millions of people all around the world. This photograph shows singers and dancers performing *Wicked* in Guangzhou, in southern China.

LONG RUNNER The musical *Wicked* premiered (first showed) on Broadway in 2003, where it is still running, and has since been staged in many other cities around the world.

BRILLIANT BACKING The chorus line is made up of actors, singers, and dancers who back up the leads and add to the razzamatazz.

TURN IT UP! The stars of a musical have to be able to act, dance, and sing. They sing in a special style, with plenty of volume and feeling, to fill the theater with sound.

THREE PARTS A musical is made up of three main parts: the music, the song lyrics, and the book (also called a libretto). The book is the storyline and what the characters say to each other between songs.

PUTTING ON A SHOW
Stage design is the way that the set and scenery are used to help tell the story, and it can include incredible special effects.

MAD HATTERS
Spectacular, colorful costumes help audiences identify each character.

CAST OF CHARACTERS
Wicked is based on some characters from *The Wizard of Oz*.

That's So **Country**

PEOPLE MIGHT LISTEN TO IT ALL OVER THE WORLD TODAY, but American country music's roots are with both the Wild West's cowboys and the southern region of Appalachia, where it grew out of folk music brought from the British Isles and Europe. Country music's simple chords and harmonies, along with its strong storylines, meant a whole lot of folks could relate to it. Formerly called "hillbilly music," by the 1920s, country music had found its way to the cities, where plenty of people also enjoyed it.

The rise of the radio in the 1920s helped to transform country folk music into a highly popular music style. Western movies also played a part, because many movies heavily featured country songs. Most country songs told a story, with musicians often singing about how things were better in the old days, cowboy culture, small-town life, and religion. The acoustic guitar, banjo, fiddle, and steel guitar all tended to show up in country songs, and the earliest country singers sang through their noses, creating an unmistakable nasal twang.

Radio shows, such as the *Grand Ole Opry*, were hugely successful and turned Nashville, Tennessee, into the heart and soul of the country music industry. The first country music stars included Fiddlin' John Carson and the Carter Family, who started recording in the 1920s. There was also Jimmie Rodgers, who some consider the first ever pop star. Famous names since then include Hank Williams, Patsy Cline, Johnny Cash, and Dolly Parton. Country music evolved and changed throughout the 20th century, and it now includes a wide range of styles, from southern rock to bluegrass to western swing and rockabilly.

THE CARTER FAMILY: GUITARIST MAYBELLE, SONGWRITER ALVIN, AND SINGER SARA

At the age of 12, Jimmie Rodgers ran away from home to join a traveling circus.

JIMMIE RODGERS'S FIRST HIT, "BLUE YODEL," SOLD MORE THAN A MILLION COPIES.

[BEHIND the Notes]

In 1925, a Nashville radio station called WSM debuted a show called *The WSM Barn Dance.* It was a variety show based on rural barn dances (traditional country dances), and featured singers and musicians as well as comedy and variety acts. In 1927, the show was renamed the *Grand Ole Opry*, poking fun at the fancy opera that was often broadcast just before it. The *Opry* became a massive hit and the longest-running radio show in the United States.

VIOLINIST ROY ACUFF AND HIS SMOKY MOUNTAIN BOYS AT THE *GRAND OLE OPRY*

+ AWESOME INSTRUMENT +
HAWAIIAN STEEL GUITAR

GUITARS WERE FIRST USED IN HAWAII IN THE 1830s, usually to play the indigenous music of the island. Then, in the 1880s, Joseph Kekuku had the idea to start sliding a comb or the back of a penknife along the strings of the guitar while it was on his knees. It created a totally different sound. Pretty soon, "steel guitars" similar to Kekuku's that used steel bars for sliders, were being produced. The Dobro brand steel guitar remains a popular country music instrument today.

▲ STEEL GUITAR

Electric lap steel guitars are designed to be played horizontally.

[TUNEFUL Terms]

Named after the Blue Ridge Mountains of Virginia and based on traditional folk songs, bluegrass became popular in the 1940s. Musician Bill Monroe is credited as being the first to put bluegrass on the map. He played the mandolin while his bandmates, the Blue Grass Boys, used other acoustic string instruments. The musicians sang in high-pitched voices and used call-and-response singing, which came out of church singing, country blues, and African-American spirituals.

BILL MONROE AND THE BLUE GRASS BOYS

 **LISTEN UP!**
CARTER FAMILY, "KEEP ON THE SUNNY SIDE"

Musical **Mania**

TECHNICALLY, MUSICAL COMEDY ORIGINATED IN LONDON IN THE 1890s, when someone combined traditionally popular theater singing acts and comedy sketches with light opera. But when musical comedy made its way to the United States and blended with American theater, a distinctive American style of musical comedy was born. By the 1920s, the performances were an extravaganza of colorful costumes and settings, dancing, songs, funny dialogue, romance, and the triumph of good over evil.

ST. JAMES THEATRE
44th ST. W. of BROADWAY   MATINEES THURS. & SAT.

A BROADWAY POSTER ADVERTISING THE FIRST PRODUCTION OF *OKLAHOMA!* IN 1943

American musical comedies tended to center around boy-meets-girl stories and include plenty of singing and dancing. Songs that proved popular could then be played on the radio, sold as printed sheet music, or be made into records. Classic American musical comedies include George Gershwin's *Lady, Be Good!* (1924) and Cole Porter's *Anything Goes* (1934).

Musical comedies, or musicals as they came to be known, were often created by two people: one who wrote the lyrics, story, and dialogue and the other who wrote the music. In 1927, composer Jerome Kern worked with the writer Oscar Hammerstein II to create *Show Boat*, a musical that combined drama, singing, and dancing in a brand-new way. Hammerstein went on to partner with the composer Richard Rodgers, and together they jump-started a golden age of musicals. Their hits are still familiar today, including *Oklahoma!* (1943), *Carousel* (1945), *South Pacific* (1949), *The King and I* (1951), and *The Sound of Music* (1959).

Rodgers and Hammerstein weren't alone. Many other indelible musicals from truly great creators appeared during the same era, including Irving Berlin's *Annie Get Your Gun* (1945), Cole Porter's *Kiss Me, Kate* (1948), and Leonard Bernstein's *West Side Story* in 1957.

IRVING BERLIN

Dorothy Fields wrote more than 400 songs for Broadway musicals and movies.

+ MUSICAL MASTER +

+ DOROTHY FIELDS +

Dorothy Fields started out working as a teacher and writer because her father didn't want her to go into show business. Before long, however, Fields was writing lyrics and selling them for $50 apiece. In 1936, she shared the Academy Award for her song "The Way You Look Tonight." Fields was an enormous success, and she is considered one of the greatest lyricists in the history of Broadway. In 1971, she became the first woman inducted into the Songwriters Hall of Fame.

[BEHIND the Notes]

Broadway is a wide avenue that runs north to south in New York City—but it's so much more than just a street. Musical theater found its way to Broadway as far back as 1866, although it really took off in the 1920s with productions called the Ziegfeld Follies. The electric lights used on theater signs earned the street its nickname, the Great White Way. Today, "Broadway" refers to any production performed at one of the forty 500-seat theaters in the area between Times Square (42nd Street) and 53rd Street.

+ MUSICAL MASTER +

+ COLE PORTER +

Cole Porter came from a wealthy family and was highly educated. But his true calling was to write some of the best loved songs of the 20th century in a series of hit musicals. His sophisticated songs tend to use humor and didn't always have a lot to do with the musicals they were in. But it didn't matter. His first hit was "Let's Do It" in 1928, and he wrote the hit musical *Kiss Me, Kate* a full 20 years later in 1948.

THE BRIGHT LIGHTS OF BROADWAY IN 1939

The Phantom of the Opera is the longest-running Broadway show.

LISTEN UP!
IRVING BERLIN, "PUTTIN' ON THE RITZ"

The Great American Songbook

THE RISE OF RADIO AND MOVIES in the 1920s meant millions of people could now hear songs that had once only been available to live audiences. Broadway musicals churned out an endless stream of popular hits, which became part of a wider American and worldwide culture. Today, beloved productions such as *The Phantom of the Opera*, *Chicago*, and *Les Misérables* have become blockbuster franchises, running for years and being turned into Hollywood movies. Maybe you're humming a hit from your favorite musical right now!

When the Great Depression hit in 1929, many songwriters left Broadway behind and headed to Hollywood. Some of them became legends, including George and Ira Gershwin, Irving Berlin, and Duke Ellington, all of whom had hit songs that became standards, or favorite tunes, many of which are performed to this day. These standards gave a new generation of superstar performers, such as Frank Sinatra, Ella Fitzgerald, and Sammy Davis Jr., a huge portfolio of material to choose from. Collectively, the songs they sang became known as the Great American Songbook.

Most of these songs were written in a fairly short period between 1920 and 1950. But when a new music style called rock and roll burst onto the scene, the songbook began to lose steam. The Great American Songbook tended to appeal to adult audiences, while rock and roll was targeted for teenagers. Because of shifts in the population after World War II, the 1950s saw a big increase in the number of teenagers—many of whom had their own money to spend on music that had been written for them. The songbook era had faded by the end of the decade.

FRANK SINATRA

ELLA FITZGERALD IN THE 1940s, SHORTLY AFTER HER DEBUT HIT "A-TISKET, A-TASKET"

+ MUSICAL MASTER +

+ GEORGE GERSHWIN +

George Gershwin was one of the greatest composers in the history of American music. When a bandleader asked him to write a piano concerto for his band, Gershwin wrote "Rhapsody in Blue." The song sounded new and different, and it combined elements from several musical styles, including jazz. Gershwin also composed with his brother Ira, and together they contributed many standards to the Great American Songbook.

Gershwin's "Summertime" is one of the most covered songs in history.

[BEHIND the Notes]

Tin Pan Alley was a district in New York City where songwriters and publishers worked. The name eventually referred to the entire American popular music industry from the late 1880s until the mid-20th century. At the time, most money in the music industry was earned by publishing sheet music. Tin Pan Alley was also the name of a song style that used catchy tunes and smart lyrics, some of which were written by top composers such as Berlin, Kern, Porter, and Gershwin.

TIN PAN ALLEY MUSIC PUBLISHERS ON 28TH STREET, BETWEEN 5TH AND 6TH AVENUES, IN ABOUT 1900

+ MUSICAL MASTER +

+ ELLA FITZGERALD +

Born in Virginia, U.S.A., Ella Jane Fitzgerald got her first break at the age of 17 when she won a competition at the Apollo Theater in Harlem, New York City. Fitzgerald scored her first hit in 1938 and became a leading singer. She went on to win 13 Grammy Awards and sell more than 40 million albums, earning the nickname the "First Lady of Song." A series of eight studio albums featuring more than 245 songs, called *The Complete Ella Fitzgerald Song Books*, has some of her best known work.

LISTEN UP!
GEORGE GERSHWIN, "RHAPSODY IN BLUE"

Songs of the
Silver Screen

HAVE YOU EVER NOTICED HOW IMPORTANT THE MUSIC IS IN YOUR FAVORITE MOVIE? Soundtracks provide emotional cues to the audience—are things about to get scary? Funny? Romantic? Much of movie music is composed specifically to match the scenes on the screen. While different countries have different musical expectations for their movies, the powerful combination of music and images can take you on a roller-coaster ride of emotions no matter where you are in the world.

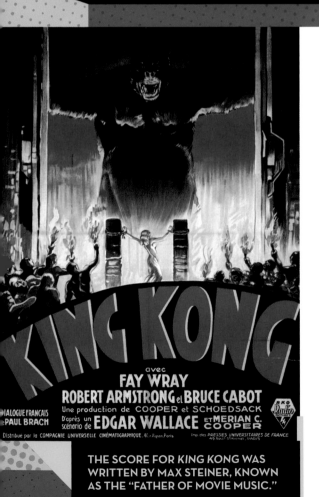

THE SCORE FOR *KING KONG* WAS WRITTEN BY MAX STEINER, KNOWN AS THE "FATHER OF MOVIE MUSIC."

The first movies were silent—no one knew how to record sound yet, so a pianist or organist played in the theater to cover up the noise of the projector. The live musician often played well-known pieces, adapting them on the cuff. Music for a movie is called a score, and the first complete movie score is thought to have been composed by Victor Herbert for a silent movie in 1916. But the first piece of original movie music was written by the French composer Camille Saint-Saëns in 1908.

When talkies—aka movies with sound—debuted, movie music became more important. Soon, composers who had made their names in classical music were trying their hands at creating movie scores. Russia's Prokofiev wrote the music for Sergei Eisenstein's films. All over the world, composers were being hired to write scores for the expanding movie industry, whether in Hollywood, Europe, or India's Bollywood. As people got used to talkies, scores became more adventurous and integral to some movies' lasting success. Bernard Herrmann wrote the unforgettable, still-gives-people-nightmares score for Alfred Hitchcock's thriller *Psycho* in 1960.

EUROPEAN IMMIGRANTS, SUCH AS ERICH KORNGOLD, WROTE THE SCORES OF MANY HOLLYWOOD MOVIES IN THE 1930s AND '40s.

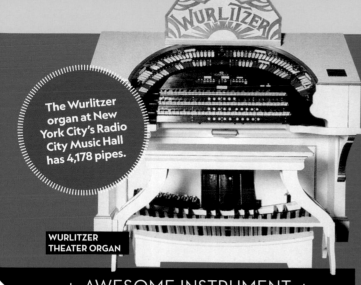

The Wurlitzer organ at New York City's Radio City Music Hall has 4,178 pipes.

WURLITZER THEATER ORGAN

+ AWESOME INSTRUMENT +
THEATER ORGAN

THE THEATER OR MOVIE ORGAN WAS INVENTED FOR THE AMERICAN WURLITZER COMPANY BY A BRITISH DESIGNER. The instrument is a pipe organ with several keyboards and a horseshoe-shape arrangement of switches that operate the pipes. Organs were perfect for accompanying movies, because they allowed for one musician to create a huge range of music and sounds, including special effects such as horses' hooves and police sirens. The organs were often placed on platforms that rose up into the theater at the beginning of a movie.

[TUNEFUL **Terms**]

India's enormous movie industry is known as Bollywood—a combination of the place-names Bombay and Hollywood—and music is a key component of nearly all Bollywood movies. Most of them include at least six songs and three dances. The first Bollywood movies had as many as 50 songs in each one. Typically, actors lip-synch (no need to be a talented vocal artist!) to songs that have been prerecorded by singers who are known as playback artists.

A DANCE SCENE FROM *KABHI KHUSHI KABHIE GHAM...*, ONE OF BOLLYWOOD'S BIGGEST HIT MOVIES

+ MUSICAL MASTER +

+ BERNARD HERRMANN +

Bernard Herrmann was a prolific American composer who wrote 49 movie scores. He was one of the first composers to use electronic music, which can be heard in his score for the 1951 science-fiction movie *The Day the Earth Stood Still*. He was a fan of 20th-century English composers and spent several months in London each year. Hermann's last score was for a 1976 film directed by Martin Scorsese.

Bernard Herrmann was inspired by the work of Charles Ives and other American composers.

 **LISTEN UP!**
KAVI PRADEEP, *"DOOR HATO AE DUNIYAWALO"*

SO MUCH HIGH-IMPACT, IMPORTANT, AND JUST PLAIN ENJOYABLE MUSIC was written in the first half of the 20th century that you could spend an entire lifetime learning about it. Here are a handful of the most influential musicians, including a country star who wore only black, a guitar superstar, and an Indian movie director turned composer.

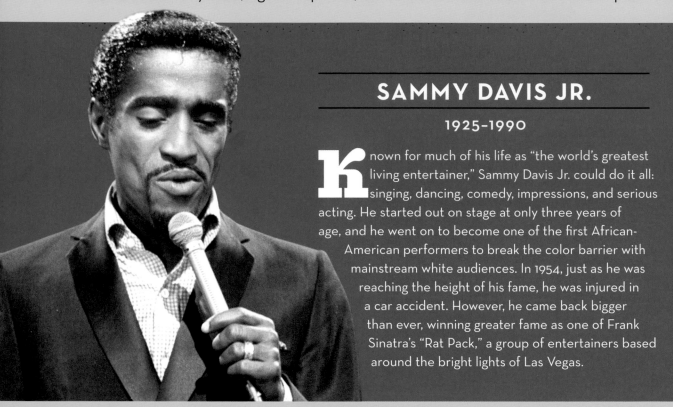

SAMMY DAVIS JR.

1925–1990

Known for much of his life as "the world's greatest living entertainer," Sammy Davis Jr. could do it all: singing, dancing, comedy, impressions, and serious acting. He started out on stage at only three years of age, and he went on to become one of the first African-American performers to break the color barrier with mainstream white audiences. In 1954, just as he was reaching the height of his fame, he was injured in a car accident. However, he came back bigger than ever, winning greater fame as one of Frank Sinatra's "Rat Pack," a group of entertainers based around the bright lights of Las Vegas.

ANDRÉS SEGOVIA

1893–1987

Until Andrés Segovia came along, the guitar had strictly been an instrument for peasants. No classical musician would be caught dead playing one. Segovia first picked up a guitar at the age of four, and as a teenager he decided to turn the guitar into a respectable instrument. He wanted it to be taught in schools and played in orchestras. At first, "serious" musicians laughed him off stage, but he eventually won everyone over with his incredible talent. Soon, composers were writing music for the guitar, and Segovia's students were spreading his ideas around the world.

RICHARD RODGERS 1902–1979
and OSCAR HAMMERSTEIN II 1895–1960

Americans Rodgers and Hammerstein joined forces in 1943 and went on to become the greatest partnership in the history of musical theater. Rodgers was responsible for the music while Hammerstein wrote the lyrics. Their first show together was *Oklahoma!* They went on to write eight more Broadway musicals. Eventually, they racked up 42 Tony Awards, 15 Academy Awards, two Pulitzer Prizes, two Grammy Awards, and two Emmy Awards. Talk about two GOATs! Before this duo, the longest run for a Broadway musical had been 700 performances. Their musicals averaged runs of 1,000 performances.

JOHNNY CASH

1932–2003

Johnny Cash grew up in rural Arkansas, U.S.A., where he first heard the country songs that inspired him for the rest of his life. Cash became known as the "Man in Black" (he always wore black when he performed, because it was easier to keep clean, he said). One of the best-selling musicians of all time, Cash has sold more than 90 million records worldwide. He is the only person so far to be inducted into the Country Music Hall of Fame, the Rock and Roll Hall of Fame, and the Songwriters Hall of Fame.

SATYAJIT RAY

1921–1992

Satyajit Ray is best known as an Indian movie director, whose movies found success with audiences in the United States and Europe. Ray had a lot of musical ideas of his own, so in 1961 he started writing his own movie music. It meant he could create the music at the same time he wrote the scripts for his movies. Ray believed music helps tell the story and provides audiences with emotional cues. He often combined Indian and Western music styles, which was unusual for Indian movies and made his movie scores unique.

BIG BANDS ELECTRIFIED DANCE FLOORS IN THE 1930s.
HERE, DUKE ELLINGTON LEADS HIS BIG BAND.

All-American
Sound

No question about it—life in the early 20th century was faster than ever before. Technology was changing and improving people's lives, and those changes came at a furious pace. While new strides in dance, theater, film, and other art forms inspired some modern music in the early 1900s, there were other important forms of American music gaining recognition. Born in African-American communities, and with deep roots in traditional African songs and dances, jazz and the blues were innovative sounds. These musical styles helped lay the groundwork for popular music to come.

Spirited Singing

MANY PEOPLE WHO CAME TO NORTH AMERICA brought music traditions with them, but none was more important to modern popular music than the slaves who were forcibly taken from Africa and brought to the United States. Enslaved people often used music to communicate and keep their spirits up. It became a form of triumph and protest; some songs were actually audio maps, guiding people to freedom. This rich musical tradition laid the groundwork for so much of the 20th century's music.

The name "spiritual" comes from the songs sung at Christian religious revival meetings of the 18th and 19th centuries. But spirituals, which differ from hymns and psalms, came to be associated with enslaved African Americans. Spirituals such as "Go Down Moses" drew on the traditions of folk tunes, the ring ritual, call-and-response singing, and repetition. The lyrics were often about Bible stories concerning slavery, freedom, and the promise of a better life to come.

White musicians attempted to write down some African-American spirituals in a collection called *Slave Songs of the United States*, and these songs first found a national audience in 1871, when a group of black singers from Fisk University in Tennessee, U.S.A., performed them on tour. Fisk University had been founded to educate African Americans, and the Fisk Jubilee Singers traveled to raise money for the school, even going to Europe. Although spirituals morphed into a more modern style in African-American churches once gospel music came on the scene, the influence of spirituals can still be heard in gospel's powerful lyrics and voices.

THE FISK JUBILEE SINGERS IN 1882

In 2009, the Fisk Jubilee Singers received a Grammy nomination for Best Gospel Performance.

[BEHIND the Notes]

Rhythmic drumming has always been an important part of West African music, especially for the ring ritual, which involved people dancing and stamping in a circle, losing themselves in the music until they reached exhaustion. Enslaved people from West Africa brought the ritual with them when they were forced to come to North America, although slave masters banned drums to prevent enslaved people from communicating secret messages. Without drums, people kept the rhythm with their hands and feet or by beating sticks together.

MUSICIANS PLAYING DJEMBE DRUMS IN MALI, WEST AFRICA

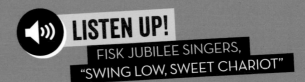

LISTEN UP!
FISK JUBILEE SINGERS, "SWING LOW, SWEET CHARIOT"

[BEHIND the Notes]

African-American spirituals were passed by word of mouth from generation to generation until after the Civil War (1861–65), when three white music collectors, William Francis Allen, Lucy McKim Garrison, and Charles Pickard Ware, tried to write down the spirituals sung by freed slaves on an island off the coast of South Carolina. The songs they noted were published in the 1867 collection called *Slave Songs of the United States*. It remains an important historical record of spirituals.

[BEHIND the Notes]

The earliest minstrel shows were clearly racist and offensive. Dating back to before the Civil War, they involved white musicians blackening their faces and performing songs and dances from African-American culture. The end of slavery after the Civil War saw black performers gradually taking over minstrel shows, turning them into a way to earn a living as a musician or entertainer. Famous musicians such as Bessie Smith and W. C. Handy started off in black minstrel groups.

SLAVE SONGS OF THE UNITED STATES WAS THE FIRST COLLECTION OF AFRICAN-AMERICAN MUSIC TO BE PUBLISHED.

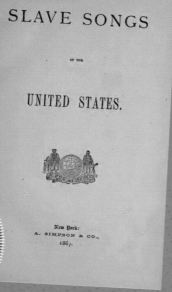

SLAVE SONGS

OF THE

UNITED STATES.

New York:
A. SIMPSON & CO.,
1867.

Slaves sometimes used spirituals as a way of passing on "coded messages" to their communities.

COMPOSER AND TRUMPET PLAYER W. C. HANDY BECAME A GLOBAL SUPERSTAR IN THE 1920s AND '30s.

Ragged Time Rhythms

RAGTIME MUSIC—THE TERM REFERS TO "RAGGED TIME," which is the unusual rhythm of this style—was made popular by African-American composer and pianist Scott Joplin. He wrote the "Maple Leaf Rag," which was published in 1899 and sold more than 75,000 copies in just six months. Imagine what sales would have been like if online ordering had been available! The song remains a standard for piano players today, along with his even more famous hit, "The Entertainer."

AFRICAN-AMERICAN PERFORMERS DANCING THE CAKEWALK IN 1901

THE SHEET MUSIC OF SCOTT JOPLIN'S "MAPLE LEAF RAG" HAD SOLD MORE THAN HALF A MILLION COPIES BY 1909.

At the turn of the 20th century, African-American music tended to use a syncopated rhythm in which different notes are emphasized to avoid a regular rhythm. This stemmed from an earlier time, when enslaved Africans developed a dance called the cakewalk, which was a way of mocking the formal dances held by wealthy slave masters. Musicians used syncopation on improvised percussion instruments and banjos to accompany the dancers. After the abolition of slavery, African-American musicians were able to play the piano, and they adopted a distinctive syncopated playing style. The left hand played the lower (bass) part with a slow rhythm while the right hand played a melody (treble) in a different rhythm.

Sheet music of ragtime pieces, which were called rags, became popular with white musicians, because they were so different from the slower, more serious music generally available at the time. The first rag to be printed was William Krell's "Mississippi Rag" in 1897, followed soon after by Tom Turpin's "Harlem Rag." Music publishers in New York promoted ragtime through sales of sheet music and piano rolls (for player pianos that automatically played notes), and, eventually, music recordings.

+ SCOTT JOPLIN +

Scott Joplin was born in Texas, U.S.A., in 1868. He became a traveling musician and performer, and in Missouri, U.S.A., he worked at the Maple Leaf Club, which inspired his most famous rag. Joplin was ambitious, writing ragtime operas and ballets, but his music was forgotten after his opera *Treemonisha* flopped. The world rediscovered him more than 50 years after his death, when the 1970s movie *The Sting* made Joplin's music popular again.

Scott Joplin was known as the "King of Ragtime."

🔊 LISTEN UP!
SCOTT JOPLIN, "MAPLE LEAF RAG"

◄ BANJO

+ AWESOME INSTRUMENT +
BANJO

THE BANJO HAS A LONG NECK AND A CIRCULAR BODY, and players pluck and strum its strings. Early on, banjos were made from skin-covered gourds and were probably inspired by a West African instrument called a *xalam*. It was first used by enslaved West Africans who were transported to the Americas. Although ragtime is mainly associated with the piano, the first ragtime recordings featured banjos.

An English physician visiting Jamaica in 1687 described the banjo as a "strum strump."

[BEHIND **the Notes**]

The cakewalk was just what it sounds like: a competitive dance that involved walking, with a cake as the prize. Invented by enslaved people, it had become a national dance craze by the 1890s. Performed to syncopated marches and, later, to ragtime music, the cakewalk was the first dance to cross from African-American to white culture. Another ragtime dance was the foxtrot, which was created by dancer Harry Fox in 1914, when he was moving to ragtime music.

HARRY FOX

Belt Out Those **Blues**

A FOUNDATION OF POPULAR MUSIC, THE BLUES CAME OUT OF AFRICAN-AMERICAN FOLK MUSIC. The term "blues" was used to describe the gloomy nature of the songs. And they really were gloomy, often telling stories about poverty, slavery, unhappy relationships, lost love, violence, racism, and death. Distinctive blues rhythm patterns can be found in a huge range of today's pop music, and some early stars, such as Bessie Smith and Robert Johnson, have become legendary blues figures.

MAMIE SMITH MADE HISTORY WHEN IN 1920 SHE BECAME THE FIRST AFRICAN-AMERICAN MUSICIAN TO RECORD A BLUES SONG.

Mamie Smith was called the "Queen of the Blues," but Bessie Smith was known as the "Empress of the Blues."

The blues started in the southern United States in the late 19th century and combined spirituals, work songs, dances, and ballads into a new musical style. The composer and musician W. C. Handy was one of the first to write down blues music, and he became known as the "Father of the Blues." He composed early hits such as "Memphis Blues" in 1911 and "St. Louis Blues" in 1914.

In 1920, a singer named Mamie Smith had a huge hit with her song "Crazy Blues." It was such a smash that it made the music industry realize there was money to be made by recording music created by and for African Americans. Another singer named Bessie Smith became a star, singing in a style known as vaudeville or classic blues. As African Americans left the South behind and headed north during the Great Migration of the 20th century, a whole new range of blues styles developed, such as the Chicago blues. This style used electric guitar and was started by Big Bill Broonzy. But the musicians Muddy Waters, Howlin' Wolf, and B.B. King made it truly popular. By the 1950s, the name had changed to rhythm and blues to widen its appeal.

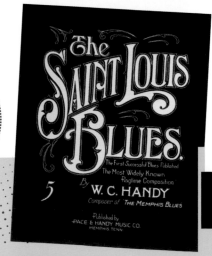

THE SHEET MUSIC FOR W. C. HANDY'S "ST. LOUIS BLUES"

BESSIE SMITH

+ MUSICAL MASTER +

+ BESSIE SMITH +

Bessie Smith was one of the most influential blues singers of the 1920s. Born into poverty in Tennessee, Smith became a popular singer in the jazzy vaudeville style, known for her glamorous flair. She had a stop-you-in-your-tracks voice, and her 1923 record "Downhearted Blues" became a best seller. By 1937, however, her career had faded. She died that year after she was injured in a car crash.

[TUNEFUL Terms]

Delta blues was an early type of country or down-home blues and took its name from the Mississippi Delta region. Many consider the region to be the birthplace of the blues, because it's where W. C. Handy first heard the style in 1903. Blues musicians traditionally handed down their know-how, allowing for one generation to inspire the next, forever linking pioneering blues musicians such as Charley Patton to later players including Robert Johnson and Muddy Waters.

MUDDY WATERS

[TUNEFUL Terms]

Most blues music follows the same pattern: the first line of both the words and music is repeated in the second line, and the third line is a response. Listen to W. C. Handy's "St. Louis Blues" for an example. The form is known as 12-bar blues, because the words and melody play out over 12 musical bars, or measures.

LISTEN UP!
ROBERT JOHNSON,
"RAMBLIN' ON MY MIND"

A Jazzy Start

THE WORD "JAZZ" MEANS UPBEAT AND LIVELY. Jazz music grew out of ragtime and mixed rhythms from West Africa with European harmonies and American marches, as well as some vaudeville and gospel singing. Although jazz has particular rhythms, harmonies, and melodies, one of its unique features is improvisation; jazz performers improvise, or make up, some of the music as they play. This artistic freedom keeps the sound fresh and is no doubt one reason why jazz is still immensely popular today.

Jazz developed throughout the southern United States, but New Orleans, Louisiana, is often said to be its birthplace. The many different cultural traditions in the city blended together to create a unique and classic style of jazz. Pioneers such as Jelly Roll Morton, who combined ragtime and jazz, and King Oliver, who gave cornet player Louis Armstrong a start in his Creole Jazz Band, were leaders of classic New Orleans jazz, also known as Dixieland. Played by an ensemble of trumpet, trombone, clarinet, piano, drums, banjo or guitar, and bass, Dixieland songs are straightforward and tuneful, and the musicians improvise as a group.

From New Orleans, jazz traveled up the Mississippi River to other cities. King Oliver and Louis Armstrong headed north and developed their own styles in Chicago, Illinois, U.S.A. Other musicians ended up in New York, New York; Kansas City and St. Louis, Missouri; and Memphis, Tennessee. Duke Ellington created a new form of big band jazz, and bandleader Paul Whiteman played music that combined jazz with classical music. When Prohibition banned the sale of alcohol in the 1920s, private clubs and dance halls started opening, and they all played the latest jazz tunes. As a result, this new music style flourished.

DAGUERRE Chicago

Dixieland jazz is also known as "traditional" or "hot" jazz.

KING OLIVER'S CREOLE JAZZ BAND POSE WITH THEIR INSTRUMENTS IN THE EARLY 1920s.

+ LOUIS ARMSTRONG +

Louis Armstrong (nicknamed "Satchmo") was born in New Orleans and started learning to play the cornet at the age of 11. When he was 12, he got in trouble and was sent to a detention center, where he improved his skills by playing in the band there. After his release, he went on to play in jazz bands and became a huge star with a series of recordings made from 1925 to 1928. He switched to trumpet and became a virtuoso, and he was also famous for his gravelly voice and for being a showman. Armstrong toured nearly every country in the world, had many hits, and appeared in many movies.

Louis Armstrong once said, "This one's for you, Rex!" to King George V during a royal performance.

+ JELLY ROLL MORTON +

Jelly Roll Morton, born Ferdinand Joseph LaMothe, learned to play the piano at the age of 10. He played in Storyville, part of New Orleans, and created a sophisticated style of jazz from ragtime, French dances, and other musical influences. Later he toured the United States and made recordings with his Red Hot Peppers band. He was a virtuoso piano player and the first great jazz musician to write his music down. His compositions helped players improvise and respond to one another.

+ AWESOME INSTRUMENT +
CORNET

A CORNET IS A BRASS INSTRUMENT WITH THREE VALVES AND IS SIMILAR TO A TRUMPET. The main difference between the instruments is the width of the tube (called a bore) that runs through them. A trumpet's bore is a uniform width, while the bore in a cornet starts narrow and becomes wider. This gives the cornet a softer, warmer sound, and it has been popular since its invention in the 1820s. Famous cornet masters include Louis Armstrong and jazz musician Bix Beiderbecke.

CORNET ⌃

LISTEN UP!
LOUIS ARMSTRONG AND THE HOT FIVE, "HEEBIE JEEBIES"

Really Big Bands

BIG BAND JAZZ USES A WHOLE LOT OF MUSICIANS, all of whom play together in a popular, entertaining style. When it first developed, the big band sound appealed to just about everyone. A New Orleans group called the Original Dixieland Jazz Band started making best-selling recordings of it as early as 1917. Big band was a part of jazz from its earliest days, and the popular style went on to conquer the country and eventually the rest of the world.

Big bands make a big, bold sound, but the number of musicians makes improvisation tricky. That's why bands tend to rely on music that has been previously arranged and rehearsed. Musicians are usually grouped together in four sections: saxophones, trumpets, trombones, and a rhythm section of piano, guitar, bass, and drums.

Jazz musicians Fletcher Henderson and Duke Ellington put together the first large-scale black jazz orchestras in the 1920s. They led the bands and also arranged the music they played. The best known big band in North America was Paul Whiteman's jazz band, which played symphonic jazz that had similarities to classical music. The main melody was played by an instrument section, and solos showcased the virtuoso playing of a musician.

Ellington found fame playing at the whites-only Cotton Club in Harlem in New York City. When the 1930s Great Depression hit, big names such as Ellington and Cab Calloway managed to continue earning a living when many other musicians fell on hard times. Around this time, William "Count" Basie developed a new swing style of big band jazz, which featured aggressive improvisation and sounded more like the blues.

CAB CALLOWAY

PAUL WHITEMAN IN THE 1920s

A big band usually has between 10 and 25 musicians.

[BEHIND **the Notes**]

The Cotton Club was opened in Harlem by gangster Owney Madden as a place to sell his illegal beer during Prohibition. The musicians and dancers were carefully chosen, young, light-skinned black people, but the customers were white, because black audiences weren't allowed inside. The club tried to give its customers the feeling of being in a plantation or jungle and portrayed black people as inferior beings. After the Harlem riots in 1935, the club moved to the Broadway theater district, but it was not a great success there and it closed in 1940.

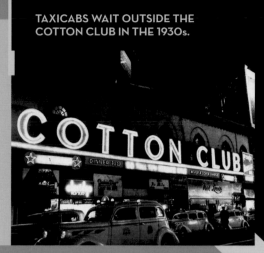

TAXICABS WAIT OUTSIDE THE COTTON CLUB IN THE 1930s.

+ MUSICAL MASTER +

+ DUKE ELLINGTON +

Edward "Duke" Ellington learned to play jazz in his hometown, Washington, D.C., and went on to become the most important bandleader in jazz. He is generally considered to be the greatest jazz composer ever and a true artistic genius. In 1927, his group became the house band at Harlem's infamous Cotton Club, and he recorded many hit tracks around the same time. Later, Ellington combined classical and jazz traditions and composed pieces about the black experience in the United States. He wrote about 6,000 compositions over his lifetime.

Duke Ellington's last words were: "Music is how I live, why I live, and how I will be remembered."

🔊 **LISTEN UP!**
DUKE ELLINGTON, "MOOD INDIGO"

[BEHIND **the Notes**]

The Harlem Renaissance was an artistic, social, and political movement in the 1920s that centered around the famous black New York City neighborhood. Author Alain Locke, who was known as the "Father of the Harlem Renaissance," called Harlem "the greatest Negro city in the world." Harlem Renaissance artists created new art, literature, dance, and music about black identity and celebrating black culture. They also pushed for civil rights and better opportunities, and musicians such as Duke Ellington and Bessie Smith were important figures within the movement.

A PROCESSION THROUGH HARLEM IN THE 1920s

Swing **Sets**

SWING MUSIC IS A TYPE OF BIG BAND JAZZ that became hugely popular dance music in the late 1930s and '40s. As the United States emerged from the Great Depression, the public wanted to be entertained. The mood-lifting music played constantly on records and the radio, and it spawned a culture with its own dances and clothing styles. Big band leaders helped bring jazz to a wider audience, moving it out of smaller, less respectable clubs from the Prohibition era and into North America's finest ballrooms.

TOMMY AND JIMMY DORSEY

Swing really took off around 1935, when the white clarinetist Benny Goodman toured with his big band. But Goodman didn't invent swing. The credit for that goes to African-American bandleader and pianist Fletcher Henderson. His band included a great lineup of musicians, including Louis Armstrong, but he wasn't a good businessman and the band broke up.

Fletcher went on to arrange music for Goodman, who had started his own dance band. Goodman produced music mostly for white audiences, which fell hard for swing. The music spread quickly and soon dance floors were crowded with young people dancing the shag and the Lindy Hop.

Swing music did not use experimentation and improvisation. It required precision and rhythmic skill. Big bands, such as those led by Glenn Miller and Tommy and Jimmy Dorsey, gave a start to famous singers including Bing Crosby and Frank Sinatra. While most big bands included only white musicians, Goodman's swing band featured both black and white musicians.

Benny Goodman was known as the "King of Swing."

BENNY GOODMAN TAKES CENTER STAGE IN FRONT OF HIS SWING BAND IN 1937.

Miller once said, "America means freedom and there's no expression of freedom quite so sincere as music."

+ MUSICAL MASTER +

+ GLENN MILLER +

Glenn Miller was an American trombonist and bandleader from Iowa, who played in a number of bands before forming his own in 1937. While his first band didn't take off, Miller's second band did, and it included some of the greatest stars of the swing era. In 1942, Miller joined the U.S. Army and put together an all-star band to entertain troops. But in December 1944, the airplane he was on vanished midflight between England and Paris. He was never heard from again.

+ MUSICAL MASTER +

+ FLETCHER HENDERSON +

Fletcher Henderson, who earned a college degree in chemistry but could not find a job because of racism, turned to music to earn a living. Henderson started a band with clarinetist Don Redman, and they decided to include many more musicians than was standard at the time. That gave them a richer sound that proved wildly popular. But Henderson fell on hard times. By 1934, instead of playing his own arrangements, he was selling them to Benny Goodman.

LISTEN UP!
GLENN MILLER, "PENNSYLVANIA 6-5000"

[BEHIND **the Notes**]

Most American homes had radios when the United States entered World War II in December 1941 (a different scenario from back in World War I). Many jazz and swing musicians joined the war effort, entertaining troops and raising spirits at a time when jazz had been banned in Nazi Germany and occupied Europe. The United Service Organization (USO) arranged concerts for soldiers all over the world, and Glenn Miller and his band played more than 300 USO shows overseas.

A USO PERFORMER SINGS TO A CROWD OF SOLDIERS ONBOARD A SHIP THAT CARRIES TROOPS.

Era of the
Big Bands

BIG BANDS ARE JAZZ ORCHESTRAS. They ruled the world of popular music in the United States and much of the rest of the world in the 1930s and '40s. Cab Calloway's band was one of the biggest; one of his songs sold more than a million copies, and he and his band played at the Cotton Club in Harlem in New York City. With costumes, cartoons, and showmanship, Calloway and his band were a whole entertainment package.

MULTIMEDIA MARVEL
With movie screens showing cartoons that danced along with the music, a visit to see Calloway's band was a real multimedia experience.

THE MAN IN THE WHITE SUIT
A white tuxedo was Calloway's signature look. See how fancy the band's clothes are, too.

SCAT STUDENT
Cab Calloway went to law school, but he always wanted to be a musician. Louis Armstrong taught him how to scat (sing nonsense words in a jazz style).

SHOWTIME!
Showmanship was a big part of Calloway's success; here, he is using props, such as an oversize book and a bag, as entertaining gimmicks.

DEPRESSION BUSTERS
This photo shows Cab Calloway's big band performing in New York City in 1938. His band was one of the few to survive and thrive during the Great Depression of the 1930s.

Cab Calloway

MAKE SOME NOISE Calloway has two pianists to make enough sound to fill a theater in an age before electronic loudspeakers were common.

HOW MANY HORNS? The horn section includes trumpeters, trombonists, saxophonists, and clarinetists.

JAZZ ORCHESTRA This big band was arranged much like a classical orchestra, with groups of instruments in rows, focused on the bandleader.

FEEL THE BEAT The double bass and the drummer are the rhythm section; they make the beat that the rest of the band follows.

Boppin' to **Bebop**

EVEN AT THE HEIGHT OF SWING, many jazz musicians were still experimenting and developing different styles. By the 1940s, yet another new, modern form of jazz had appeared on the scene. Known as bop or bebop, star performers such as Dizzy Gillespie, Charlie Parker, and Thelonious Monk would improvise together, responding to each other's sounds instead of sticking to a melody. The freedom of this new music felt refreshing and exciting for all involved—everyone from the performers to the listeners loved it.

BILLIE HOLIDAY IN 1948, THE YEAR IN WHICH SHE FIRST PERFORMED AT NEW YORK'S CARNEGIE HALL

While big bands had taken over popular music, small jazz groups hadn't disappeared, especially in big cities. Musicians such as clarinetist Sidney Bechet, pianist Fats Waller, and singer Billie Holiday would jam together, playing in an unrehearsed way. They performed for fun and simply to see what would happen. Musicians playing in this style had to be experts on their instruments, so they could think fast and keep up as the music morphed.

By the early 1940s, many jazz fans had grown bored of swing, because it had all started to sound the same; it had become too mass-produced. Duke Ellington complained, "Jazz is music, swing is business." People were looking for the next big thing in jazz, and the alto saxophonist Charlie Parker provided it by creating bebop. Bebop used a more complicated rhythm than traditional jazz, and it relied on constant improvisation and long solos. Parker and a group of musicians that included trumpeter Dizzy Gillespie, pianist Thelonious Monk, and drummers Max Roach and Kenny Clarke, played bebop at Minton's Playhouse in New York.

THELONIUS MONK (LEFT) AT MINTON'S PLAYHOUSE IN 1947

+ MUSICAL MASTER +

+ CHARLIE PARKER +

Charlie Parker was a jazz saxophonist who lived a short but amazing life. He grew up in Kansas City, Kansas, and went by the nickname "Yardbird," (and sometimes just "Bird"), although no one knows why. Some people believe it was because he loved eating chicken, and in Kansas, some people called chickens yardbirds. After Parker moved to New York, he helped to invent bebop. Unfortunately, his music wasn't widely appreciated at the time, and he died young, at just 34 years old.

+ MUSICAL MASTER +

+ BILLIE HOLIDAY +

Hands down, Billie Holiday was one of the greatest jazz singers ever. Holiday had been inspired to sing jazz and blues after hearing Bessie Smith and Louis Armstrong. Between 1935 and 1942, she made more than a hundred records. Her unique singing style almost mimicked jazz musician solos, and she used her voice to create emotional, often sad, songs. Holiday performed with many big bands and artists, including Benny Goodman and Duke Ellington. She died at the young age of 44 in 1959.

Billie Holiday auditioned to be a dancer, but instead wowed everyone with her singing.

 LISTEN UP!
CHARLIE PARKER, "ORNITHOLOGY"

+ DIZZY GILLESPIE +

John "Dizzy" Gillespie was an American trumpet player from South Carolina. He was known for his "balloon cheeks," puffing them out as he played, and for his custom trumpet with a bell that was bent at 45 degrees. He played in Cab Calloway's band, and jammed at Minton's Playhouse, a New York City nightclub, in the early 1940s. In 1944, Gillespie became director of the first bebop band, and shortly afterward he teamed up with Charlie Parker to record the first bebop records.

The Sound of **Cool**

AS GROUNDBREAKING AS BEBOP WAS, it could be tough to listen to. So by the late 1940s, many people were glad to have a new style of jazz come along. Cool jazz aimed to build on the best of swing. Whereas bebop was loud, exciting, and almost completely improvised, cool jazz featured relaxed melodies, was quieter, and was more structured. Cool jazz was also called West Coast jazz.

Chet Baker was a great trumpet player. His solo from "My Funny Valentine" became one of his signature tunes.

CHET BAKER

Miles Davis was an American trumpeter who had played bebop but wanted to strike out on his own path. So he put together a group of nine musicians, including a French horn player and a tuba player—instruments that had never before been heard in jazz bands. The group made a series of recordings in 1949 called "Birth of the Cool," putting a new style of jazz out in the world.

Some described the sound of this gentler, more laid-back style of jazz as being like "a cool glass of water." It definitely matched California's relaxed vibe. Musicians played what was written down in cool jazz, so there was less improvisation, although the music was often more experimental than bebop. Key musicians of this style included pianist Dave Brubeck, Shorty Rogers, Chet Baker, and John Lewis. Lewis's band, the Modern Jazz Quartet, played quiet jazz and often mixed in influences from classical music.

MILES DAVIS PLAYING THE TRUMPET AT THE "BIRTH OF COOL" RECORDING SESSIONS

★ MUSICAL MASTER ★

★ JUNE CHRISTY ★

June Christy, born Shirley Luster in Illinois, helped to launch the vocal side of the cool jazz movement. Christy recorded some hits with Stan Kenton's Orchestra in the 1940s, but she is best known for her work with arranger Pete Rugolo on the album *Something Cool* in 1954. Her warm, clear voice set the standard for cool jazz singing.

🔊 LISTEN UP!
DAVE BRUBECK QUARTET, "TAKE FIVE"

June Christy never learned to sight-read, but memorized all her parts after a quick run through at the piano.

★ MUSICAL MASTER ★

★ MILES DAVIS ★

Born in Illinois, Miles Davis studied music in New York, where he also played in early bebop bands in jazz clubs. Davis explored a variety of styles and experimented with electronic instruments and electric amplification for his trumpet. His 1959 album *Kind of Blue* is considered to be the greatest jazz album ever, and one of the best albums of all time, period. Its hypnotic sound has influenced generations of musicians ever since.

[BEHIND the Notes]

During the 1950s, the U.S. government sent American jazz musicians on tour in Communist countries in an effort to promote democracy through culture. Legendary stars such as Louis Armstrong and Dizzy Gillespie joined West Coast musicians, including Dave Brubeck, in the effort. In 1958, the Dave Brubeck Quartet played 12 shows in Poland, where the Communist government had banned jazz. Brubeck told fans: "No dictatorship can tolerate jazz. It is the first sign of a return to freedom."

DAVE BRUBECK AT THE PIANO WITH HIS BANDMATES IN 1962

107

Free From **Rules**

FREE JAZZ IS JUST THAT: FREE. Emerging in the late 1950s, it was an attempt to break down the rules that had governed jazz before. Musicians can play anything they want whenever they want. Sometimes there is no rhythm at all, and players don't need to play specific chords. Musicians still react to each other, but they aren't restricted by conventions. This lets them explore their emotions through the music, and no one has to worry about making weird sounds with their instrument. In fact, it's encouraged!

ORNETTE COLEMAN

Ornette Coleman invented a whole new way of composing, which he called "harmolodics."

Musicians were experimenting with free jazz as early as the 1940s, but the style really developed in the late 1950s and made its presence known with the release of Texas saxophonist Ornette Coleman's album *Free Jazz* in 1961. John Coltrane, another saxophonist who had been playing bebop, became one of the most influential free jazz musicians, along with pianist Cecil Taylor. Free jazz musicians intentionally make strange sounds with their instruments, wailing, squawking, and squeaking their way through pieces that sometimes sound like explosions of noise. One version of free jazz is called "energy music" or just "noise." All players improvise at the same time, making unconventional sounds to express ideas and feelings.

Later versions of free jazz include the work of Sun Ra, who staged colorful performances and claimed to have traveled to Saturn. Free jazz was not limited to the United States; different versions sprung up all over the world, from Great Britain's Jamaican-born alto saxophonist Joe Harriott to the Ganelin Trio from the Soviet Union. The Brotherhood of Breath, a band of South African exiles in London, mixed free jazz with kwela music from their South African townships.

FREE JAZZ MUSICIAN SUN RA WROTE AND STARRED IN A MOVIE CALLED *SPACE IS THE PLACE*.

+ MUSICAL MASTER +

+ JOHN COLTRANE +

John Coltrane was a star saxophonist in Miles Davis's quintet. At one time, Coltrane had struggled with addiction, but he overcame it and turned into the best known player of free jazz, as well as a cultural icon for black artists. His style was described as having "sheets of sound." Later in his career, he used Eastern and African influences in his jazz. Coltrane's most famous recording was the 1965 album *A Love Supreme*.

The term "kwela" is thought to be taken from the Zulu word for "climb."

LEMMY "SPECIAL" MABASO PUTS ON A STREET SHOW IN 1959.

[BEHIND the Notes]

Visual art and music have long been connected, and the arrival of bebop and free jazz strengthened those ties even further. The performers of these musical styles were less interested in having smash hits and more focused on creating audio art. Around the same time, new painting styles were also developing. American painter Jackson Pollock listened to jazz while he worked, and he compared the way he made his splash paintings to the way a jazz musician improvises.

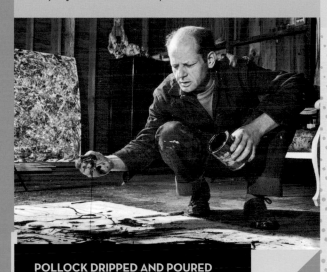

POLLOCK DRIPPED AND POURED PAINT ALL OVER A CANVAS TO CREATE HIS SPLASH PAINTINGS.

🔊 LISTEN UP!
JOHN COLTRANE, "MY FAVORITE THINGS"

[TUNEFUL Terms]

Kwela is an African jazz style that started in South Africa in the late 1950s and early 1960s, when South African kids tried to re-create the American big band jazz sounds they'd heard. They played cheap penny whistles and simple one-string basses made from tea chests. Also called tin whistle jive or penny whistle jive, kwela music spread throughout southern Africa. Leading players included Spokes Mashiyane (see p. 113), Lemmy "Special" Mabaso, and Daniel Kachamba.

Funky **Fusions**

JAZZ IS A CONSTANTLY CHANGING, EXPANDING STYLE OF MUSIC, and fusion—the mixing of musical styles—has been key to its development. In the United States, jazz has been fused with rock, funk, and classical music, as well as Indian and African music styles. One of the most popular forms of fusion blends traditional jazz with Latin American dances and rhythms, particularly those from Cuba. When Latin jazz came on the scene, it created yet another entirely new style of music.

Jelly Roll Morton said that jazz was born with a Spanish tinge, thanks to the Latin influence in New Orleans culture. Even some early jazz tracks, such as W. C. Handy's 1914 "St. Louis Blues," hint at the reach of habanera, a Cuban dance music. But the height of Latin jazz fusion came in the 1930s and '40s, when Latin musicians including Juan Tizol, Mario Bauzá, Chano Pozo, and Machito and His Afro-Cubans collaborated with American jazz artists, such as Dizzy Gillespie and Duke Ellington. After the 1940s, two main schools of Latin jazz emerged: Afro-Cuban and Brazilian. Both were inspired by popular Latin American dances. Afro-Cuban Latin jazz includes salsa, merengue, mambo, and cha cha cha, while Brazilian Latin jazz includes bossa nova and samba. Latin jazz draws on different rhythms from traditional American jazz, and musicians play different instruments, including maracas, bongos, and five-key flutes. Percussion is especially important in jazz fusion.

However, fusion isn't limited to Latin styles. John Coltrane used Indian and Middle Eastern sounds to create a different fusion style. And Joe Harriott and Indian violinist John Mayer combined their styles to create Indo-jazz fusion.

A BRAZILIAN SAMBA DANCER

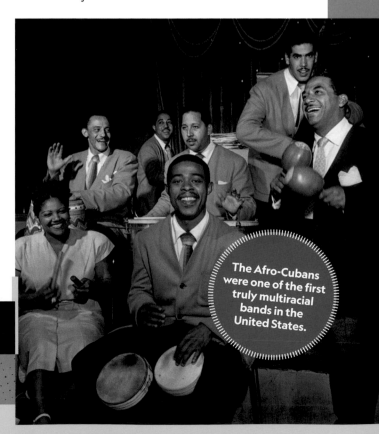

MACHITO (FAR RIGHT) WITH HIS BAND THE AFRO-CUBANS

The Afro-Cubans were one of the first truly multiracial bands in the United States.

[TUNEFUL **Terms**]

Bossa nova is a Brazilian music and dance style. It's a kind of soft samba with a strong melody and harmony and less percussion. Bossa nova has connections to Brazil's beachy vibe as well as its political protests. The term first appeared in the 1959 song "Desafinado" by Antônio Carlos Jobim. In 1962, a bossa nova craze hit North America, and João Gilberto's tune "The Girl from Ipanema" became the world's second most played song (after The Beatles' "Yesterday").

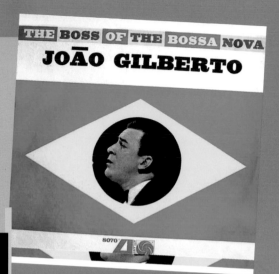

THE BOSS OF THE BOSSA NOVA
JOÃO GILBERTO

THE COVER OF JOÃO GILBERTO'S 1962 ALBUM, *THE BOSS OF THE BOSSA NOVA*

+ **MUSICAL MASTER** +

+ **TITO PUENTE** +

Ernesto "Tito" Puente was born in New York and is of Puerto Rican descent. He was a bandleader and arranger who was also a master of the timbales (drums used in Latin American music). But he also played vibraphone, piano, congas, bongos, and saxophone. His band helped spread the craze for mambo, cha cha cha, and other Latin jazz styles. Puente became known as the "King of Latin Music."

🔊 **LISTEN UP!**
TITO PUENTE, "OYE COMO VA"

+ AWESOME INSTRUMENT +
SAMBA PERCUSSION

IN BRAZIL, SAMBA IS THE MUSIC OF CARNIVALE, and its percussion instruments are designed to be both lightweight (so that they can be easily carried around) and extra loud (to help draw crowds). Samba instruments include the *surdo*, a large bass drum that's hit with a padded beater; the *caixa*, a snare drum with wires on top of the drum head to make a louder tone; the *repinique*, a double-headed drum tuned to a high pitch; and the *chocalho*, a shaker with metal jingles.

National Samba Day takes place on December 2 in Brazil.

CHOCALHO ➤

THE MOST SIGNIFICANT BLUES AND JAZZ MUSICIANS WERE ALSO SOMETIMES THE MOST UNPREDICTABLE. B.B. King loved his guitar so much he rescued it from a fire and then named it, while Frank Sinatra recorded a song with a dog. Here are some more unforgettable folks from the jazz world.

B.B. KING

1925–2015

Riley King was B.B. King's real name. He grew up as a cotton farm worker and fell in love with the guitar at an early age. Along the way, he earned the nickname "Blues Boy," which got shortened to B.B. He was so attached to his guitar that he once ran into a burning building to rescue it. He later named the guitar Lucille. Together, they had many hits, including "The Thrill is Gone." He went on to become one of the world's most famous and respected blues guitarists, and rock musicians such as Eric Clapton and U2 waited in line to work with him.

FRANK SINATRA

1915–1998

The legendary Frank Sinatra was probably the most popular American singer of all time. As a young man in the swing era (see pp. 100–101), Sinatra sang with big bands in a jazzy style and scored a slew of hits. His popularity dimmed after World War II, leading to a loss of recording contracts. But Sinatra made a huge—and lasting—comeback in the 1950s, and he even became an Oscar-winning movie star.

SPOKES MASHIYANE

1933–1972

South African musician Spokes Mashiyane's record company called him "King Kwela," because he was one of the inventors of kwela (see p. 109). Mashiyane came up with some truly original sounds that no one else could replicate, including playing a penny whistle by putting the end of it inside his mouth against his cheek. He first learned to play music while tending his father's cows; he'd blow through the reeds in the fields to make sounds. Later on, he switched to the saxophone and invented another new type of jazz, called mbaqanga, which became even more popular than kwela.

ROBERT JOHNSON

1911–1938

Robert Johnson was a blues musician who grew up in the Mississippi Delta. His recordings "I Believe I'll Dust My Broom" and "Ramblin' on My Mind" used a rhythmic bass line called a walking bass, which influenced later guitarists such as Elmore James and Eric Clapton. Legend holds that Johnson came by his considerable musical talent by making a deal with the devil at a crossroads.

JOÃO GILBERTO

b. 1931

João Gilberto Prado Pereira de Oliveira helped create bossa nova, the world's most popular style of Brazilian music (see p. 111). Gilberto first picked up a guitar at the age of 14, wanting to come up with new rhythms and even a new way to sing. Eventually, a fellow musician recognized his talent, which helped Gilberto go on to become a massive bossa nova star in Brazil and the United States.

THE OWNER OF THE RECORDED WORK RESERVED UNAUTHORISED PUBLIC PERFORMANCE BROADCASTING AND COPYING OF THIS RECORD PROHIBITED

Tamla Motown

TRADE MARK OF MOTOWN RECORD CORPORATION

45 R.P.M.

TMG 892

2A

573

own Record

Corporation

HE'S MISSTRA KNOW IT ALL
(Stevie Wonder)

STEVIE WONDER
Arranged & Produced by
Stevie Wonder

MADE IN GT BRITAIN

A STEVIE WONDER SINGLE RELEASED IN 1974 BY THE
LEGENDARY MOTOWN RECORD LABEL (SEE P. 119)

5

1950–1970s

Play It Loud

A retha. Elvis. James Brown. The Beatles. The second half of the 20th century would see the rise of gospel, rhythm and blues, and rock and roll. Not to mention some of the most influential musicians of all time. The increased cultural and commercial power of teenagers (and their wallets) turned pop music into a colossal industry that dominated music around the world. Music remained a way to give voice to different political and protest movements, and for people from every corner of the globe to share their stories.

We've Got the **Blues**

BILLBOARD MAGAZINE FIRST USED THE TERM "RHYTHM AND BLUES" IN A 1949 ISSUE, and the style's history is nearly as complex as the music itself. Rhythm and blues usually describes a blues and jazz fusion—upbeat jazz sounds and soulful rhythms that reflected the shifting social and economic landscapes of the time, combined with jumping beats that are just right for dancing. A lot of folks were just looking to have a good time in the 1950s, and rhythm and blues fit the bill.

Rhythm and blues quickly proved popular. It was easier to listen to than bebop and it had a strong beat. It included a wide range of styles, including blues-style jazz (also known as soul jazz) with wailing saxophones and blues vocals, played by bands led by Louis Jordan, Joe Liggins, and Johnny Otis. Another style was New Orleans jazz, which had a swinging shuffle beat played by the likes of the famous pianist Fats Domino. And then there was the electric blues guitar with its jumping beats, played by leading musicians such as T-Bone Walker and B.B. King.

Rhythm and blues was, above all, music for people to dance to. The style is best remembered today as being one of the main influences on rock and roll. The rhythm and blues music played by performers such as Bo Diddley, Chuck Berry, and Little Richard was not so different from later rock and roll. In the 1980s, the term rhythm and blues got shortened to R&B, but it still described a wide range of music, from smooth soul to driving funk.

FATS DOMINO

SAXOPHONIST LOUIS JORDAN'S TYMPANY FIVE WAS ONE OF THE HOTTEST SOUL JAZZ BANDS.

During the 1940s, Louis Jordan's Tympany Five had 18 No. 1 hits on the R&B charts.

+ AWESOME INSTRUMENT +
SAXOPHONE

INVENTED BY ADOLPHE SAX IN 1840, the saxophone is a woodwind that's played with a reed in the mouthpiece. The instrument is made of brass and has a strong, pure sound. The sax is easy to pick out in a crowd of instruments, which makes it popular among both marching and big bands. It's a key instrument in rhythm and blues songs, with saxophonists honking and wailing in powerful solos that sent audiences into a frenzy.

SAXOPHONE ▶

▲ MOUTHPIECE WITH REED

BEHIND the Notes

Unfortunately, racism and segregation in the music industry continued well into the second half of the 20th century, and still sometimes occurs today. Many people believed that black artists should perform for only black audiences. Recorded African-American music was referred to by the offensive term "race records" until 1949, when "rhythm and blues" finally replaced it. Soul replaced the term rhythm and blues in the late 1960s, but the shorter term R&B made a comeback and is still used today.

Bo Diddley played the violin as a child, and he claimed it influenced his distinctive guitar style.

LISTEN UP!
BO DIDDLEY, "WHO DO YOU LOVE"

+ MUSICAL MASTER +

+ BO DIDDLEY +

Bo Diddley, born Elias Otha Bates in 1928, grew up surrounded by gospel and blues, and was inspired by the famous singer John Lee Hooker to take up the guitar. Diddley's playing had a driving beat and a hard-edged guitar sound, and he was an enormous influence on later rock and roll artists, from Buddy Holly to Jimi Hendrix. Diddley is sometimes known as "The Originator," although he complained about the lack of credit he got for his work, saying, "I opened the door for a lot of people, and they just ran through and left me holding the knob."

BO DIDDLEY'S FAMOUS SQUARE-EDGED GUITAR WAS SPECIALLY MADE FOR HIM IN THE 1950s.

Giving **Praise**

GOSPEL AND SOUL ARE CLOSELY RELATED AFRICAN-AMERICAN MUSIC STYLES, and they're both linked to rhythm and blues. The soulful sounds of the singers and the heartfelt songs about overcoming everyday struggles are meant to fill performers and listeners alike with hope. Gospel developed out of the African-American spiritual tradition, and soul grew out of gospel. This popular music style produced some of the most powerful voices in music history, including Ray Charles, Aretha Franklin, and Otis Redding.

Gospel music is rooted in African-American Protestant church music, and it developed at a time when many black Americans left the South to move to northern cities. Gospel songs are known for their syncopated rhythms, and often include call-and-response singing—when a leader sings a line and a chorus answers. Gospel became an important part of the civil rights movement during the 1960s, when stars and activists such as Mahalia Jackson joined the protests.

Gospel had a big influence on what popular music sounded like. Songs and singers were described as having "soul" when they used gospel styles, such as melisma—when a musician sings one syllable or word while moving through several notes—and glissando—when notes slide into one another quickly. Gospel notes can also be bent, or change pitch.

After rhythm and blues faded, soul dominated popular black music. There were many different regional soul styles and record labels, including the legendary Stax in Memphis, Tennessee, and Motown Records in Detroit, Michigan. Soul music included everything from sweet love songs to strong political tunes with clear messages, such as "Say It Loud: I'm Black and I'm Proud," by James Brown.

Motown had more than 180 No. 1 hit singles worldwide.

BERRY GORDY, FOUNDER OF MOTOWN RECORDS, POSES WITH DIANA ROSS (RIGHT) AND THE SUPREMES.

+ MUSICAL MASTER +

+ ARETHA FRANKLIN +

Aretha Franklin first sang in church—her father was a reverend and her mother sang and played the piano. Franklin grew up listening to Mahalia Jackson, so she had plenty of gospel influence. She became known as the "Queen of Soul," and is one of the style's icons. Her voice had a huge range and she was a talented piano player. In 1987, Franklin became the first woman to be inducted into the Rock and Roll Hall of Fame.

[TUNEFUL **Terms**]

Originally founded in Detroit in 1959, Motown took its name from the words "motor" and "town." A sign above its door read "Hitsville U.S.A." The first black-owned record company, Motown became one of the greatest record labels of all time. The label's roster included an incredible number of stars, ranging from Diana Ross, Smokey Robinson, and the Jackson 5 to Marvin Gaye, Stevie Wonder, and Gladys Knight.

MARVIN GAYE'S "I HEARD IT THROUGH THE GRAPEVINE"—A NUMBER ONE HIT IN 1968

+ MUSICAL MASTER +

+ MAHALIA JACKSON +

Martin Luther King, Jr., said of Mahalia Jackson that a voice like hers "comes along once in a millennium."

Born in New Orleans in 1911, gospel singer Mahalia Jackson moved to Chicago as a teenager and played a big part in popularizing gospel outside of the church. Her signature song, "Move On Up a Little Higher," was recorded in 1947 and became the first gospel song to sell one million copies. In 1961, she sang at President Kennedy's inauguration. Jackson was a key figure in the civil rights movement, accompanying her friend Martin Luther King, Jr., on marches and singing at his funeral.

🔊 LISTEN UP!

ARETHA FRANKLIN, "RESPECT"

Everybody Rock!

ROCK AND ROLL BURST ONTO THE SCENE IN 1956 WITH THE SONG "ROCK AROUND THE CLOCK," and music was never the same again. An immediate hit with young people from all backgrounds, rock and roll gave rise to a whole new youth culture. Many adults were horrified by the new music—they disapproved of its strong beat and thought it was downright dangerous. But knowing that parents disapproved of the latest songs probably just helped make rock and roll even more popular.

The success of "Rock Around the Clock" unleashed a wave of rock and roll hits, but the style had actually started well before 1956. A disc jockey in Cleveland, Ohio, U.S.A., claimed to have used the phrase as early as 1951 to describe a style of rhythm and blues that appealed to both white and black audiences. While rock and roll started as a fad, within a few years, teens had turned it into the most profitable music in the world. The term "rock and roll" covers a lot of different styles. But a classic rock and roll song is a series of choruses that follow a 12-bar blues progression (see p. 95). The songs drew heavily from rhythm and blues and also borrowed from gospel, country, and swing. While there were several early rock and roll stars who turned into larger-than-life legends, including Little Richard and Elvis Presley, few are considered more influential to the style than Chuck Berry. With his onstage dance moves and his unique fast and electrified combination of blues, country, and rhythm and blues, he helped to define rock and roll for years to come.

LITTLE RICHARD

John Lennon of The Beatles once said, "If you tried to give rock 'n' roll another name, you might call it 'Chuck Berry.'"

CHUCK BERRY SCORED HIS FIRST HIT IN 1955. "MAYBELLENE" BLENDED A RHYTHM AND BLUES BEAT WITH COUNTRY GUITAR LICKS.

+ MUSICAL MASTER +

+ ELVIS PRESLEY +

Elvis Aaron Presley, born in Tupelo, Mississippi, started out as a country singer before making three hit records in 1956: "Heartbreak Hotel," "Hound Dog," and "Don't Be Cruel." Presley, with his deep, soulful voice and hit songs, fundamentally changed popular culture. He went on to become "the King," one of the biggest music stars in the world, and an American icon. Elvis spent much of the 1960s making Hollywood movies, but in 1968, he burst back onto the music scene with the legendary *'68 Comeback Special* TV show.

BEHIND **the Notes**

The invention of cheap transistor radios helped put music into the hands of young people—literally. Now they could listen to whatever they wanted. Radio disc jockeys (DJs) also became a hugely influential part of the music industry—they had the power to make or break songs, depending on how often they played them on air. DJs were so important that bribery scandals broke out—more than one DJ faced accusations of accepting money from record companies to play certain songs.

AN EARLY TRANSISTOR RADIO

🔊 LISTEN UP!
CHUCK BERRY, "JOHNNY B. GOODE"

+ AWESOME INSTRUMENT +
ELECTRIC GUITAR

THE FIRST ELECTRIC GUITARS APPEARED IN THE 1930s. They became popular with bands because they let one guitarist make as much noise as an entire horn section. An electric guitar has electronic pickups under each string that convert a string's vibration into an electrical signal, which feeds into an amplifier and out of a loudspeaker. Guitars with solid bodies were developed in the late 1940s and '50s, including the legendary Fender Stratocaster and the Gibson Les Paul. Many guitarists preferred their cleaner sound to that from hollow-body guitars.

ELECTRIC GUITAR ➤

The world's most expensive guitar, a Fender Stratocaster, was sold for $2.7 million in 2004.

Folksy **Protests**

THE 1960s WERE AN ERA EXPLODING WITH CULTURAL AND POLITICAL UPHEAVAL, from Vietnam War protests to the fight for civil rights. Music became a key ingredient of many social movements, with some singers using traditional folk songs to share their messages. Bob Dylan was one of the greatest protest folk artists of the time. Many of his early songs became anthems for more than one movement. Dylan's lyrics focused on political and social unrest, reminding everyone that "the times they are a-changin'."

1960s superstars Paul Simon and Art Garfunkel met at elementary school.

Folk music wasn't a new genre—it is known to have existed since well before the 19th century. And because it was once the popular music of the day, the folk revival of the mid-20th century definitely didn't replace rock and funk. But it did offer folk musicians the chance to bring back traditional song styles and add their voices to protest movements.

Folk songs were usually played on acoustic guitars and tackled the important social and political challenges of the era. Audiences filled with counterculture hippies and Vietnam War protesters embraced the meaningful tunes. Singers typically wrote their own songs, which helped to popularize the role of the singer-songwriter (something The Beatles would adopt a bit later). Woody Guthrie performed his pro-union songs, while Pete Seeger, Joan Baez, and Bob Dylan shared anti-war tunes. For some, it was a huge surprise when, in 1965, Bob Dylan put down his acoustic guitar and plugged in his electric instrument, but the move helped create a different style of folk rock. Other artists such as Simon and Garfunkel drew inspiration from folk while still creating rock and popular music.

BOB DYLAN

SIMON AND GARFUNKEL

JIMI HENDRIX AT WOODSTOCK

BEHIND the Notes

In August 1969, the Woodstock Music and Art Fair took place in upstate New York. The festival was billed as "three days of peace and music," and when all was over, nearly half a million people had shown up. The musical lineup included some of the greatest rock and folk acts of all times, with performances by stars such as Jimi Hendrix, Janis Joplin, and Jefferson Airplane. Woodstock turned out to be a key moment for a generation of music fans and activists.

 **LISTEN UP!**
BOB DYLAN, "THE TIMES THEY ARE A-CHANGIN'"

 + MUSICAL MASTER +

+ BOB DYLAN +

Bob Dylan, born Robert Allen Zimmerman in Minnesota, U.S.A., was a follower and fan of the traditional folk singer Woody Guthrie. Dylan created his own original talking blues style of folk singing, and took it to New York in 1961. He started out playing in clubs and eventually became a leading civil rights champion and protest singer. When he made the switch to electric instruments, he became a rock star and even made religious music. In 2016, Dylan received the Nobel Prize in Literature for his songwriting.

Joan Baez was already a star when she met Bob Dylan and helped to launch his career by inviting him on stage.

 + MUSICAL MASTER +

+ JOAN BAEZ +

Joan Baez is an American folk singer and political activist. Like her friend Bob Dylan, Baez started playing in small venues, where she sang traditional ballads and accompanied herself on guitar. She helped turn the gospel song "We Shall Overcome" into an anthem of the civil rights movement by performing it at marches and rallies. Between 1965 and 1975, Baez focused on her political activism instead of her music career, although she made a comeback in the late 1970s as a folk-rock singer.

JOAN BAEZ AND BOB DYLAN

123

Rocking the Greatest **Stage**

THE BIGGEST ACTS IN ROCK AND POP LIKE TO PLAY ON THE BIGGEST STAGES. Concerts in giant stadiums date back to The Beatles and before, but it was in the 1970s and '80s that stadium rock became the biggest noise in music. Bruce Springsteen and other leading acts can fill stadiums with thousands of screaming fans. Bruce and the E Street Band are shown here strutting their stuff in Milan, Italy, in 2016 on the European leg of the River tour.

MONITORS These are speakers aimed at the musicians, so they can hear themselves above the roar of the crowd—much bigger speakers will be aimed at the audience.

STANDING ROOM ONLY Right in front of the stage is the best place to find hardcore fans who love to jump around.

WITH THE BAND Fans buy T-shirts and other stuff with the name and logo of the band; wearing them at the concert shows their support.

LET THERE BE LIGHT
Lights and special effects can be used in time with the music to help create a great show.

SPORTS STADIUM Normally, this stadium hosts the AC Milan and Internazionale soccer teams, but when a big artist like Springsteen comes to town, it's time to rock out.

ELECTRIC GUITAR
A small instrument can make a stadium-filling sound when it is plugged into a colossal sound system.

ON A PEDESTAL The band has to be on a raised stage so that everyone can see them.

CALL AND RESPONSE
Imagine how it feels to be on stage and have 60,000 people sing your lyrics to you!

THE GREATEST SHOWMAN Bruce Springsteen is one of the greatest front men in rock—he knows how to work up a crowd.

The British **Are Coming!**

WHILE THE ROCK AND ROLL OF THE 1950s WAS FIRMLY ROOTED IN AMERICAN SOIL, the 1960s also saw a wave of British music crash onto North America's shores. Led by legendary bands, such as The Beatles and The Who, this British invasion (as it was called) changed music forever. Many American artists were inspired by the Brits' catchy melodies and intriguing lyrics. Along with record-breaking crowds of devoted fans, British bands brought a new idea of what pop music—that's popular music—could be.

THE BEATLES

The Beatles appeared in five movies, including *A Hard Day's Night* and *Yellow Submarine*.

The early days of British rock and roll weren't especially exciting. But there was a thriving underground scene and a handful of genuine hits. Some bands played a style known as skiffle, a combination of blues, jazz, and country, using homemade instruments to make their sound.

One skiffle band based in Liverpool, England, called themselves the Quarrymen, but they later decided to change their name to The Beatles. Maybe you've heard of them? The band first found fame in Great Britain, but Beatlemania quickly spread across the Atlantic. By 1964, they occupied the top five spots in the *Billboard* singles chart. They became singer-songwriter legends, putting out entire albums of hits. An almost-constant stream of British bands followed, including The Rolling Stones, The Kinks, and Van Morrison, which helped make the 1960s a golden era for rock music. And the British invasion inspired American artists to step up their game, with bands such as The Beach Boys and The Monkees pushing new boundaries.

PETULA CLARK HAD 15 U.S. TOP 40 HITS IN A ROW FROM 1965.

+ MUSICAL MASTERS +

+ THE BEATLES +

They joined forces in the 1950s, but the band formed by John Lennon, Paul McCartney, and George Harrison wasn't known as The Beatles until 1960. (Drummer Ringo Starr joined them later). Band manager Brian Epstein, looking to improve the band's image, got them mop-top haircuts, and soon enough they had a record deal. The Beatles' hits broke records all over the world and set trends that completely revolutionized music. The band officially broke up in 1970, but their music is still popular today.

Pete Townshend of The Who was one of the first rock musicians to smash his guitars onstage.

LISTEN UP!

THE BEATLES, "CAN'T BUY ME LOVE"

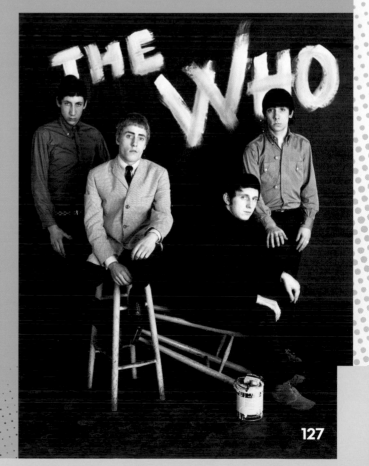

+ MUSICAL MASTERS +

+ THE WHO +

The English rock band The Who (Roger Daltrey, Pete Townshend, John Entwistle, and Keith Moon) were a major part of the British invasion. Inspired by Pop Art painters such as Roy Lichtenstein, they developed a unique sound that mixed hard rock with experimental music. The Who were especially famous for their high-energy live shows, in which Townshend and Moon would smash up their instruments, and for creating "rock operas"—albums that told a story through songs and music, such as the massive 1969 hit *Tommy.*

Rocking the Blues

BLUES ROCK USES THE STRUCTURE AND RHYTHM OF THE BLUES, but with the amplified instruments that rock relies on. It first emerged in the early 1960s, and in the hands of a number of groups, such as The Rolling Stones, the style found devoted and lasting fans. With its electric guitars, bass, and drums, not to mention its strong rhythms and powerful vocals, blues rock is still popular today.

The Rolling Stones are easily one of the most famous bands on the planet, and they're also one of the longest running. Guitarist Keith Richards and lead singer Mick Jagger were longtime friends who discovered they both liked the blues and rock and roll. Back in the early 1960s, the blues wasn't well known in Britain, but The Rolling Stones latched onto the style and combined it with rock and roll influences, such as Chuck Berry's music. The Stones played their first gig in 1962 with electric guitars, giving their music a heavier, more rhythmic sound. It was a departure from most early blues players who used acoustic instruments.

Also taking their cue from American blues, British band The Yardbirds had a succession of hits in the mid-1960s. Meanwhile, Eric Burdon, lead singer of The Animals—a band formed in northeast England—proved to have a powerful R&B voice in the 1960s and had huge blues rock hits.

◀ **ELECTRIC GUITAR**

THE ROLLING STONES ON A U.S. TOUR IN 1967

+ MUSICAL MASTER +

+ ERIC CLAPTON +

The British rock and blues musician Eric Clapton was seen as a guitar hero early in his career. His impressive tone and control of his instrument are hallmarks of his playing—he can weave his melodies around a singer's words with ease. He is a superb improviser and a master at distorting the notes he plays. Clapton is the only person ever inducted into the Rock and Roll Hall of Fame three times.

Eric Clapton launched his career playing with The Yardbirds, earning the nickname "Slowhand."

 **LISTEN UP!**

THE ROLLING STONES, "LITTLE RED ROOSTER"

+ AWESOME INSTRUMENT +
HARMONICA

The harmonica is the world's best-selling instrument. In the United States alone, more than 40 million have been sold.

THE HARMONICA, ALSO KNOWN AS THE BLUES HARP, is a mainstay in many blues and blues rock songs. Singers tend to play the instrument between verses, blowing into it to add an expressive, almost voicelike sound to any song. Its sound is produced by blowing into the instrument to make metal reeds inside it vibrate. Many American blues musicians are known for playing harmonica, including Little Walter and Howlin' Wolf. But the instrument often shows up in rock, pop, and soul songs—Stevie Wonder is famous for "blowing the harp," too (see p. 138).

< HARMONICA

STEVIE WONDER

Get Funky

FUNK MUSIC DEVELOPED STRAIGHT OUT OF SOUL IN THE LATE 1960s, using strong bass lines and complex rhythms. It often featured gospel-style vocals and lyrics that touched on everything from politics to having fun. Funk music is designed to be danced to with strong beats, blasting horn sections, and heavy bass line melodies. When funk hit the club dance floors in the 1970s, it ended up blending with soul and Latin music, and disco was born.

Bootsy Collins was just a teenager when he found fame as the bassist in James Brown's band, the J.B.s.

BASS GUITARIST BOOTSY COLLINS BRINGS THE FUNK IN 1978.

James Brown's album *Say It Loud: I'm Black and I'm Proud*, released in 1969, is widely considered the first funk record, and it pointed to a new direction in black politics as well as music. Funk became more widespread in the 1970s, when bands such as Sly and the Family Stone, KC and the Sunshine Band, and The Meters brought their own signature grooves to the party. Drum rhythms and guitar were especially important in funk, and the influence of William "Bootsy" Collins—the bass guitar player in Brown's band—can be heard in his songs, such as "Super Bad."

A simplified version of funk, disco has a strong repetitive bass drum pattern on each beat. The soundtrack of the movie *Saturday Night Fever* was a sensation in 1977, and the disco craze exploded around the world. Although disco edged out funk and other forms of soul music, later on, hip-hop artists would find inspiration in funk's rhythmic patterns.

SATURDAY NIGHT FEVER

LISTEN UP!
STEVIE WONDER, "SUPERSTITION"

TUNEFUL Terms

Funk had a big influence on the African musical style Afrobeat, which mixed traditional music from the Yoruba people of Nigeria with Western jazz and funk. The Nigerian musician Fela Kuti, who became known as the "King of Afrobeat," developed the sound with his drummer Tony Allen during the 1960s and '70s. Afrobeat groups often include more than 15 musicians, with plenty of brass and percussion. And the lyrics of Afrobeat songs are often political, using call-and-response to share the message.

BEHIND the Notes

First airing in 1970, *Soul Train* was one of the longest-running nationally syndicated television shows in American history and the first to prominently feature African-American acts and dancers. It was an influential part of black culture, featuring the hottest music, fashion, and dance moves. Don Cornelius was the executive producer and host of *Soul Train*, and he ended every show with the words, "I'm Don Cornelius, and as always in parting, we wish you love, peace, and soul!"

★ MUSICAL MASTER ★

+ JAMES BROWN +

James Brown was born in South Carolina, U.S.A., and started as a gospel singer. Before long he was playing rhythm and blues and soul, but then he helped popularize funk, creating more than 800 songs. Brown believed that the black community should be proud of being black. His unforgettable high-energy performances often included a preaching style of singing and amazing dance moves. As a singer, composer, arranger, and bandleader, he became known as the "Godfather of Soul." He inspired countless performers who came after him.

SOUL TRAIN DANCERS IN 1970

131

Sitar **Stars**

THE SITAR IS A STRINGED INSTRUMENT WITH A LONG NECK that's traditionally played in South Asian classical music. Its resonating sound first became popular in the West in the late 1960s when The Beatles lead guitarist George Harrison looked to Eastern culture for musical inspiration and spiritual guidance. Harrison took lessons with sitar master Ravi Shankar, whom he described as "the godfather of world music." Shankar soon became a household name around the world.

Brian Jones learned how to play the sitar from Harihar Rao, who was a student of Ravi Shankar.

The name "sitar" comes from the Persian word *sehtar,* meaning "three strings." Muslim rulers first introduced the instrument to India; in their courts Hindu musicians learned to play the sitar, making it a key instrument for performing classical Hindu music.

Twentieth-century Western audiences first had the chance to hear the sitar at a show created by Indian dancer Uday Shankar and Russian ballerina Anna Pavlova. The two toured Europe and North America with a band of Indian musicians, including sitar master Allauddin Khan. Tagging along for the trip was Shankar's younger brother, Ravi, who would become the world's most famous sitar virtuoso.

When George Harrison became Shankar's student, he and other musicians created fusions of Hindustani music with rock and jazz. The sitar can be heard on several Beatles songs, including "Norwegian Wood" and "Tomorrow Never Knows," and in 1966, Brian Jones of The Rolling Stones played it on "Paint it Black." The rest of the decade saw hundreds of songs featuring the sitar, although the craze had died down by 1970.

BRIAN JONES (LEFT) PLAYING SITAR ON THE ROLLING STONES HIT "PAINT IT BLACK"

+ AWESOME INSTRUMENT +
SITAR

THE MODERN SITAR HAS A LARGE BODY MADE OF A GOURD cut in half and a long neck that has metal frets and between 18 and 21 strings. A player plucks the strings with a wire plectrum twisted around their index finger. Typically accompanying the sitar are the tabla (a pair of drums) and tambura (another string instrument with a long neck). The patterns of scales and notes played on sitars are called ragas.

SITAR ➤

After his death, Ravi Shankar was honored with a Grammy Lifetime Achievement Award in 2013.

+ MUSICAL MASTER +

+ RAVI SHANKAR +

Ravi Shankar was born in Varanasi, India, and spent seven years training under sitar master Allauddin Khan, the chief court musician of the Maharaja of Maihar. Shankar invented new kinds of sitar music and even changed the design of his instrument. Throughout his career, he gave concerts around the world, performing into his late seventies. In the early 21st century, Shankar's daughter Anoushka became a well-known sitar player.

[BEHIND the Notes]

Ragas are the key to Indian classical music. They are a mixture of scales and melodies, and each raga has a particular pattern of notes. Musicians pick one to use as a basic pattern and then improvise around it. There are around 500 different ragas, although new ones are always being invented while others die out. Each raga is associated with a different time of the day, special occasion, or mood. For instance, the raga called Rag Desh is linked to late evenings in the rainy season.

SITAR PLAYERS PERFORM A RAGA

 **LISTEN UP!**
RAVI SHANKAR AND GEORGE HARRISON, "PRABHUJEE"

Rock Styles

DURING THE 1970s, ROCK MUSIC STARTED TO DEVELOP MANY DISTINCTIVE STYLES. Musicians were constantly looking for new directions and exploring all kinds of influences, which led to lots of new types of rock, including prog rock and glam rock. Rock had always embraced youthful freedom and rebellion. But now, it set out to shock the world with explosive guitar and drum sounds, outrageous costumes, and bad behavior.

In the 1970s, some fans and critics had come to view rock musicians as true artists, because they wrote and performed their own songs. Some bands made concept albums that were organized almost like symphonies, such as *The Lamb Lies Down on Broadway* by Genesis. These albums tell a story in the same way that the program music of Romantic classical music (see p. 45) does. This kind of rock was known as prog (short for "progressive") rock, and it grew out of other types of rock, such as psychedelic, folk, and jazz rock.

Meanwhile, glam rock also came on the scene, another new style that moved rock toward a more popular music sound. British musicians such as Marc Bolan of T. Rex and David Bowie were experimental artists who blended their own original music and wore outlandish, theatrical costumes. They paved the way for other artists such as Freddie Mercury of Queen, Slade, and Roxy Music. Glam rock never really caught on across the Atlantic, but American acts such as Alice Cooper and the New York Dolls had some success.

Bowie was born David Jones, but changed his last name to avoid confusion with Davy Jones of The Monkees.

GENESIS

DAVID BOWIE

BEHIND the Notes

Concept albums were often double albums that featured complicated images on the foldout cover, turning the entire package into a work of art. The covers helped tell the story and establish the world of the album before anyone even listened to the music on the records inside. Artist and designer Peter Blake's cover for The Beatles album *Sgt. Pepper's Lonely Hearts Club Band* was an early example of high-impact cover art.

SGT. PEPPER'S LONELY HEARTS CLUB BAND, RELEASED BY THE BEATLES IN 1967

+ MUSICAL MASTERS +

+ PINK FLOYD +

Pink Floyd was a British rock band whose original lineup included Syd Barrett, Nick Mason, Roger Waters, and Rick Wright (Barrett was later replaced by David Gilmour). They started as leaders of the psychedelic rock style, using light shows at their performances to create what they called "a total environment of light and sound." Their biggest album, *The Dark Side of the Moon,* was a huge hit on both sides of the Atlantic in 1973. The band also made the hit concept album and movie called *The Wall.*

Joan Jett was the first woman to own her own record label, called Blackheart Records.

+ MUSICAL MASTER +

+ JOAN JETT +

Joan Jett was born Joan Larkin in Pennsylvania, U.S.A., in 1958. Inspired by glam rock and artists, Jett formed an all-woman rock band called The Runaways in the mid-1970s. The Runaways were a huge hit when they played in Japan, and Jett went on to have a successful solo career in the 1980s, scoring a big hit in 1982 with "I Love Rock 'n' Roll" with her backup band the Blackhearts.

LISTEN UP!

PINK FLOYD, "WISH YOU WERE HERE"

Irresistible **Indipop**

ALTHOUGH THE TERM INDIPOP IS SOMETIMES USED to describe all the popular music of South Asia, the region has hundreds of different styles of popular music, so the Indipop label usually refers specifically to Indian pop dance music. It's generally based on songs from Bollywood movies, which are known as *filmi* (see p. 85). The lyrics, usually sung in Hindi, mostly tell love stories set to irresistible dance beats.

For most of the 20th century, Indipop songs were versions of traditional Indian songs, such as ghazals (a kind of poetry in the Urdu language) or *qawwali* (songs from the Sufi religion), which used less improvisation and were played on Western instruments.

Most Indipop was from hit Bollywood movies, and the songs were produced by just a handful of composers and big record companies. The first Indipop song probably came from the Ahmed Rushdi filmi "Ko Ko Korina" in 1966. Playback artists became Indipop's main stars.

But the introduction of cassette tapes led to major changes in South Asia's pop music. Hundreds of small record labels and thousands of performers could suddenly showcase their work easily. They created songs in an amazing range of styles, such as pop ghazal, which features simplified Urdu songs and a soft string accompaniment, and pop bhajan, which is a form of traditional Hindu religious songs. More recently, Western influences on Eastern pop music can be heard in newer styles, such as Hindi pop and Gujarati rap.

SINGER APACHE INDIAN CREATES A UNIQUE STYLE OF REGGAE BY BLENDING JAMAICAN, ASIAN INDIAN, AND WESTERN BEATS.

+ LATA MANGESHKAR +

Lata Mangeshkar started working as a playback singer in Bollywood in 1947, and she may be the most recorded artist in history, making songs in dozens of different languages and styles. For a period during the 1950s and '60s, Mangeshkar recorded as many as five songs a day. Her younger sister Asha Bhosle is also a huge playback star and became the first Indian singer to be nominated for a Grammy.

TUNEFUL **Terms**

Originally a music and dance style from the Punjab region of India, bhangra was sung and danced by men and featured drumming on a dhol, or barrel drum. Then the cassette tape was born, and bhangra's popularity spread like never before. In 1980s Britain, bhangra was fused with dance music and Jamaican dancehall ragga to create what's known as British bhangra. The dance and rap style has proved popular in India, too.

TRADITIONAL BHANGRA DANCERS PERFORM AT THE SIKH NEW YEAR FESTIVAL OF VAISAKHI.

LISTEN UP!
LATA MANGESHKAR, "AAJA RE PARDESI"

The sale of recorded cassette tapes peaked in the United States in 1990, with 442 million sold.

BEHIND **the Notes**

Cassette tapes were slim plastic boxes that contain reels of recording tape. They're cheap and easy to make, but they're also simple to copy and sell illegally. Copying and selling official recordings of music is called piracy. Not only is piracy a form of stealing, and therefore illegal, but it almost always denies recording artists the chance to earn money from the sales of their work. Hindi pop star Alisha Chinai made the best-selling Hindi album of all time, *Made in India*, which sold 4.5 million copies. However, half the sales were pirated, which meant she earned nothing from them.

AN INDIAN MARKET TRADER SELLING CASSETTE TAPES

137

THE 1960s AND '70s PRODUCED AN INCREDIBLE GROUP OF MUSICAL ARTISTS, many of whom made lasting cultural impact. Talented musicians such as Stevie Wonder and Fela Kuti used their voices to campaign for political change. Performers including David Bowie and Janis Joplin made people think twice about traditional gender roles. It was an era of pushing boundaries that also created some magical music.

FELA KUTI

1938–1997

The legendary musician and political activist Fela Kuti used music to battle injustice and poverty in his home country of Nigeria in West Africa. While Kuti's parents sent him to England to study medicine, he ended up focusing on music, inventing his own version of funk that blended James Brown-style music with African styles, such as highlife (see p. 158). Considered by some to be an enemy of the Nigerian government, Kuti and his family survived several attacks, but he kept making his music. Although he didn't live to see it, in 1999 Nigerians achieved the end of military rule.

STEVIE WONDER

b. 1950

Stevland Hardaway Judkins was born blind in Saginaw, Michigan, U.S.A. After learning to make music by playing along with the radio on a harmonica his uncle gave him, he was signed by the Motown record label at just 11 years old. His first No. 1 hit came when he was only 13. Billed as "Little Stevie Wonder" at the time, Motown offered him an allowance of $2.50 a week. Since then, Wonder has become one of the best-selling artists of all time, and he has effected important cultural change, including helping to make Martin Luther King, Jr.'s birthday into a national holiday.

THE BEACH BOYS

Formed 1961

The Beach Boys created a new American sound called California rock, making songs full of vocal harmonies with lyrics about surfing, driving, and girls. Later on, they made more ambitious concept albums, including *Pet Sounds* (1966), which is often cited as the best album ever made. The creative force behind The Beach Boys was Brian Wilson, while other original members included his brothers, Dennis and Carl, their cousin Mike Love, and friend Al Jardine. Brian Wilson has publicly said that he had bouts of mental illness and stopped touring or making music, but he began performing regularly again in 2004.

DAVID BOWIE

1947–2016

Pop stars who want to stay successful have to keep up with changing tastes, and no one was better at reinventing himself than David Bowie. Bowie was born in London, England, U.K., and he became a rock star who specialized in creating different looks and styles throughout his career. One of his most famous inventions was the character Ziggy Stardust, a rock star from another planet. Bowie helped start a long list of different musical styles, including punk, new wave, Goth rock, the New Romantics, and electronic music (see pp. 144–147).

JANIS JOPLIN

1943–1970

Janis Joplin came from a small town in Texas, U.S.A., where she never seemed to fit in. Joplin ran away from home to become a folk singer and ended up in San Francisco, California, where she heard about a band that needed a singer. With her big, bluesy voice, Joplin soon became a star and recorded her own albums. She was a dynamic singer who could perform both loud and intense rock songs and quiet folk songs. She was a huge inspiration for women in rock.

LADY GAGA, ONE OF THE MOST ORIGINAL POP STARS OF THE 21ST CENTURY, PERFORMS
LIVE DURING HER MONSTER BALL STADIUM TOUR.

Pop Goes the Music

Part of the appeal of pop music is how fresh and new it sounds. Since the 1970s, there has been a steady supply of new styles and stars—from punk, reggae, and heavy metal to modern country, hip-hop, and EDM. So what will the future of music sound like? Some people think it's already here, full of unexpected mash-ups and genre-bending artists. And whether it is the latest streaming app or a new hit that layers in the voice of a musician from the past, new technologies keep us on our toes when it comes to how we hear, buy, and engage with music and the artists who perform it.

Reggae Rhythms

INVENTED IN THE ISLAND NATION OF JAMAICA, reggae features a slow bass rhythm and a relaxed, easy-going sound. The style originated in the late 1960s, but found fame worldwide in the 1970s thanks to the brilliance of musician Bob Marley, whose music is still popular today. Reggae developed out of the music styles ska and rock steady, and later, it would lead to the creation of dub, dancehall, and ragga. Reggae song lyrics often discuss social issues, such as poverty and racism.

The musical roots of reggae stretch back to a type of folk music called *mento,* which was popular in Jamaica, an island in the Caribbean, beginning in the late 19th century. After World War II, young Jamaicans loved American rhythm and blues, but when rock squeezed out R&B in the 1960s, Jamaicans created ska, their own musical style that blended rhythm and blues with mento. Jamaica had recently gained independence from Britain, and ska became its new national music. Ska bands often sang about the harsh reality of everyday life in Jamaica's poor cities.

Some music producers created rock steady by experimenting with slowing down ska's tempo (or speed) and bass guitar to set the riddim. Riddim is a musical term that comes from the Jamaican Patois pronunciation of the English word "rhythm," and it's used in reggae, dancehall, and other styles to describe the instrumental part of a song. When the tempo got even slower, the music became reggae. The word "reggae" was first used in the 1968 song "Do the Reggay," by the Maytals, but Bob Marley popularized the style.

Reggae Month is celebrated in Jamaica in February, the month in which Bob Marley was born.

A REGGAE SOUND SYSTEM

DESMOND DEKKER HAD ONE OF THE EARLIEST REGGAE HITS, "ISRAELITES," IN 1968.

+ MUSICAL MASTER +

+ BOB MARLEY +

Bob Marley was born in Jamaica in 1945 and became a guitarist, singer, and writer. As a teenager, he learned to play ska, and then he came up with his own style of rock steady and early reggae. In 1972, he started recording with the major label Island Records and adjusted his sound so it had a wider appeal. It was not long before he was an international star. Marley used his inspirational lyrics to defend freedom and human rights wherever he performed.

DANCERS AT A REGGAE STREET
PARTY IN KINGSTON, JAMAICA

[TUNEFUL **Terms**]

Reggae is easy to identify, partly because it uses offbeats. The beat is the regular, rhythmic pulse that creates a framework for a piece of music. Every bar or measure of music has a set number of beats. If you count 1-2-3-4, that sets a four-beat rhythm. Count faster and the tempo increases. Reggae has a steady, chopping rhythm made by the guitar playing short, single chords on the second and fourth beats, or offbeats, of every bar. A four-beat rhythm that emphasizes the first and third beats is playing onbeat.

LISTEN UP!

BOB MARLEY, "NO WOMAN NO CRY"

Lee "Scratch" Perry sometimes created drum effects by burying microphones at the base of a palm tree.

LEE "SCRATCH" PERRY

[TUNEFUL **Terms**]

Dub is a music style that remixes record tracks, adding sounds, vocal effects, and sometimes spoken words to create a unique version of a song. The style began with Jamaican music engineer Osbourne Ruddick, also known as "King Tubby." Producer Lee "Scratch" Perry perfected dub. The style let Jamaican DJs mix their own original versions of existing songs. Many styles of music have been inspired by dub, including rap, hip-hop, dancehall, dubstep, and drum and bass.

Metalheads

HEAVY METAL TAKES ITS NAME FROM THE LOUD AND DISTORTED GUITAR PLAYING that is featured in this style. Guitarists often use long solos to show off their skills, and heavy metal song lyrics and performances tend to be dark, if not downright menacing. The band Led Zeppelin helped create heavy metal, and later the style developed into many other versions, including glam rock, thrash rock, and nu metal. Warning: Heavy metal music can be loud enough to damage your hearing!

Heavy metal was inspired by hard rock, and Jimi Hendrix was one of the first to be credited with playing in the style. But the term "heavy metal" was first used in the 1969 song "Born to Be Wild" by the band Steppenwolf. Metal bands usually rely on drums and guitar sounds known as power chords. Many early heavy metal songs had dark and serious themes. A group of three bands came to be known as the holy trinity of heavy metal: Led Zeppelin, Black Sabbath, and Deep Purple. Their ominous music featured brooding guitar riffs, thundering bass, pounding drums, and soaring vocals.

When heavy metal music reached North America after the mid-1970s, some of it changed into a more popular type of music called glam or hair metal. The name came from the flowing locks of bands such as KISS, Guns N' Roses, Bon Jovi, and Poison. Hair metal music tended to be happier, often focusing on love. But thrash metal acts such as Metallica and Megadeth also thrived, and they stuck to the original harder and darker side of heavy metal music.

In 1977, Marvel Comics published an issue presenting the KISS band members as superheroes.

KISS

[BEHIND the Notes]

An amp, or amplifier, is an essential piece of equipment for most pop music, especially heavy metal. An amplifier boosts the signal from an electric instrument and creates a loud sound when it is fed into a speaker. Rock music amps are usually combination units, with a portable loudspeaker box that contains all of the devices needed to turn guitar string vibrations into powerful sounds. Amps are worth it, because the best heavy metal music is the loudest!

+ MUSICAL MASTERS +

+ LED ZEPPELIN +

The legendary English rock band Led Zeppelin was formed in 1968 by guitarist Jimmy Page, vocalist Robert Plant, keyboardist and bass guitarist John Paul Jones, and drummer John Bonham. Jones and Bonham created a heavy bass sound, while Page played guitar sounds that became instantly recognizable and Plant sang in a powerful bluesy style. The band produced hard rock and heavy metal songs, but also some acoustic folk rock, on classic albums such as *Led Zeppelin IV* and *Physical Graffiti*.

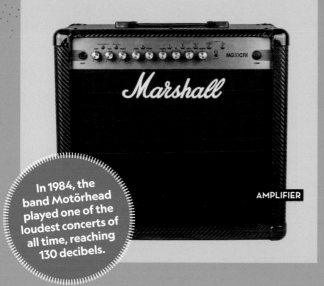

In 1984, the band Motörhead played one of the loudest concerts of all time, reaching 130 decibels.

AMPLIFIER

LISTEN UP!
THE JIMI HENDRIX EXPERIENCE, "VOODOO CHILD"

[TUNEFUL Terms]

Drawing inspiration from the solos of virtuoso musicians in both classical music and jazz, many 1970s heavy metal, hard rock, and prog rock artists incorporated guitar solos as key elements of their music. Jimi Hendrix was known for his incredible solos, and he modeled them on the showmanship of Chuck Berry. Guitar heroes such as Jimmy Page, Eric Clapton, Eddie van Halen, and Slash would follow.

EDDIE VAN HALEN

Such a **Punk**

PUNK ROCK IS ALL ABOUT ATTITUDE—USUALLY A REBELLIOUS ONE! Punk is an aggressive music style that was a reaction to the softer rock and disco music of the mid-1970s. Punk musicians did not need to be virtuosos, or even necessarily be able to sing in tune. It was all about screaming lyrics and playing loud. As long as they were willing to shock an audience, just about anyone could be a punk rock performer. Punk eventually led to new wave and musicians who experimented with electronic sounds.

The band Blondie was named after the nickname of their lead singer, Debbie Harry.

DEBBIE HARRY, LEAD SINGER OF BLONDIE

By the mid-1970s, rock fans were restless, accusing stars of selling out to make big bucks. Soon, the idea of going back to the basics, and playing short, high-energy songs with just guitar and drums took hold. A new art and fashion movement known as punk was gaining popularity, and music quickly joined the punk party. Punk musicians did not have to play well, because their music did not follow any rules. They often just turned the volume way up on their amps and let it rip. Although they might not have wanted to admit it, a lot of famous punk rock bands also happened to have talented musicians, including The Clash, Ramones, and Siouxsie and the Banshees.

New wave was originally just another name for punk, but it later referred to bands that came after punk. New wave groups still had the raw and loud sounds of punk, but they applied a little more musical skill. They also blended other styles to create unique music. Blondie mixed punk with pop, while The Police drew inspiration from reggae. Talking Heads used world music to help make their sound.

THE CLASH

BEHIND the Notes

Fashion was a key part of the punk movement, from clothes to hair to makeup. Some bands' managers even worked with famous fashion designers to create their looks. Punks showed off their independence by customizing clothes. Ripped T-shirts and jeans, torn-up army gear, chains, zippers, and safety pins were all staples of the punk image. Heavy boots, body piercings, and out-there spiky hairstyles in a rainbow of colors completed the look.

PUNKS IN LONDON WITH SPIKY MOHAWK HAIRSTYLES

+ MUSICAL MASTERS +

+ RAMONES +

Formed in 1975, the Ramones were a punk rock band from New York City. The four members—Dee Dee, Joey, Johnny, and Tommy Ramone—all took the same last name and adopted cartoonlike characters. Their real names were Douglas Colvin, Jeffrey Hyman, John Cummings, and Thomas Erdelyi. The Ramones wrote punk versions of classic rock and roll songs that were short, and played loud and fast. Their first album was called *Ramones* and had 14 tracks, but it was just 30 minutes long.

The Ramones were the first punk band to be inducted into the Rock and Roll Hall of Fame.

 **LISTEN UP!**
THE CLASH, "SHOULD I STAY OR SHOULD I GO"

147

What's Your **Tribe?**

AS THE 1980s DAWNED, THERE WERE SO MANY DIFFERENT MUSIC STYLES that some fans grouped themselves into "tribes." People who belong to the same tribe like listening to the same music, wearing similar clothes, and behaving in a similar way. Today, perhaps because the internet allows us to instantly access any music we want to hear, tribes don't exist in the same clear-cut way. But back in their heyday, they formed around music genres from Gothic rock to New Romantic to indie rock and grunge.

Imagine yourself living in the 1980s. Some tribes would listen to music played on electric guitars. Other tribes followed bands that used electronics, or that staged spectacular performances. Of all the tribes, Goths might be the best known. Post-punk and new wave music inspired the style Gothic rock, which blended horror movie imagery with gloomy songs. Goth musicians often had pale skin, dark hair, and wore dark and dramatic makeup, and their tribe took on the same look. Gothic rock led to later acts such as Marilyn Manson.

The early 1980s saw the rise of the New Romantics, who were inspired by the over-the-top fashions of the Romantic period. Post-punk bands such as Duran Duran and Culture Club made showy, theatrical songs and aimed to make money from their music. A related style called electropop or synth pop that used synthesizers found inspiration from disco, with bands such as Depeche Mode and Pet Shop Boys. Yet another tribe followed with indie rock, which included bands that released music on small, independent record labels and initially avoided synthesizers and electronic sounds. Indie acts, such as The Smiths and the Pixies, would later inspire Seattle grunge bands such as Nirvana and Pearl Jam.

PIXIES

Although the press labeled Adam Ant a New Romantic, he did not like the term, and called himself a "punk rocker."

ADAM ANT

+ AWESOME INSTRUMENT +
SYNTHESIZER

A SYNTHESIZER IS AN ELECTRONIC MUSICAL INSTRUMENT THAT USUALLY HAS A KEYBOARD. It can imitate other instruments. The first synthesizers were made in the 1920s, but in 1956, a company called RCA Victor produced an electronic piano that would look familiar today. The first computer-technology synthesizers were made by Yamaha in the 1980s, and they became common in pop music, especially dance music.

▼ YAMAHA DX7 SYNTHESIZER

+ MUSICAL MASTERS +

+ SIOUXSIE +
AND THE BANSHEES

Siouxsie and the Banshees was an English punk and later Gothic rock band led by Siouxsie Sioux, whose real name is Susan Ballion. She became one of the first female punk singers and performed a punk version of the Lord's Prayer in 1977. Her dark black hair, vampire-style makeup, and strong stage presence were a huge influence on Goth culture. Goth was inspired by punk but rejected its angrier side, so it was sometimes known as positive punk.

LISTEN UP!
THE SMITHS,
"THIS CHARMING MAN"

[TUNEFUL Terms]

Grunge started out as a mixture of slow punk and heavy metal music played by a band called the Melvins. Indie rock bands from Seattle and beyond during the late 1980s were then called grunge. Grunge rockers played amplified electric guitars like heavy metal bands but did not perform solos, have big hair, or wear tight clothes. These bands included Pearl Jam, Soundgarden, Mudhoney, and Alice in Chains. Nirvana's 1991 track "Smells Like Teen Spirit" was the biggest grunge hit, and its front man, Kurt Cobain is now seen as a rock legend.

Kurt Cobain didn't realize that Teen Spirit was a popular deodorant when he titled his hit "Smells Like Teen Spirit."

NIRVANA'S KURT COBAIN

149

Sisters Start Doin' It
for Themselves

DESPITE ITS PEPPY SOUND, A LOT OF POP MUSIC WAS NOT POSITIVE OR EMPOWERING FOR WOMEN. In the 1980s, that began to change as a wave of strong female artists burst onto the scene, making feminist rock, soul, and pop—music about women showing their strength and taking control. Some of these musicians were stars who had been standing up for women since the 1960s, such as Aretha Franklin. Others were new artists who became megastars, including Madonna and Whitney Houston.

ARETHA FRANKLIN

CYNDI LAUPER

ANNIE LENNOX

Pop music has often focused on what's happening in society at the time, whether it was a demand for civil rights or protesting a war. One of the most important cultural movements for social change in the 20th century was feminism—the demand for women's rights on the basis that men and women are equal. Aretha Franklin released her anthem "Respect" in 1967, but when she recorded "Sisters Are Doin' It for Themselves" with the Eurythmics nearly 20 years later, its message of empowering women was still new and noteworthy.

Many other trailblazing female musicians followed in Aretha's footsteps, such as Gloria Estefan (see p. 165), Annie Lennox, Pat Benatar, and Whitney Houston. But in the 1980s, it was Madonna who became a highly influential—and top-earning—female artist. Through her image and music, she preached a message of strength and confidence. Other important 1980s artists, such as Cyndi Lauper, had huge hits with songs about accepting yourself and fighting against prejudice.

★ + MUSICAL MASTER +

+ MADONNA +

Madonna Ciccone is an Italian-American singer and dancer who was often called the "Queen of Pop." She is known for constantly changing her sound and image. Considered a 1980s pop music icon for her many hit albums and videos, Madonna has carefully controlled and crafted her long career, but she has never shied away from controversy. Along with a string of hit singles and record-breaking tours, Madonna has also acted in and directed movies. She continues to use her fame as a platform for social causes.

🔊 **LISTEN UP!**
CYNDI LAUPER, "GIRLS JUST WANT TO HAVE FUN"

Whitney Houston sang "The Star-Spangled Banner" at the 1991 Super Bowl when she was only 27 years old.

★ + MUSICAL MASTER +

WHITNEY
+ HOUSTON +

The daughter of gospel singer Cissy Houston and cousin of soul legend Dionne Warwick, Whitney Houston became one of the biggest-selling female artists of all time, breaking the color barrier for women in pop and inspiring other stars, such as Mariah Carey and Janet Jackson. She was famous for her incredible voice, which had range and power, and her singing style, including her use of melisma (singing one syllable or word while moving through several notes). She also starred in several movies and produced the film *The Princess Diaries*.

Get **Hip** With the Beat

HIP-HOP IS HUGELY POPULAR ALL OVER THE WORLD TODAY as a cultural, artistic, and music movement. Hip-hop started in a poor New York City neighborhood in the 1970s, and its roots go deep into African-American and Caribbean cultures. Bringing together rap, DJing, dance, and graffiti or street art, hip-hop is not only a type of music but a way of life. The rapper and DJ Lovebug Starski is often credited with giving hip-hop its name—he claimed that when he got stuck for words, he'd improvise with "hip, hop, the hip …"

The term "rap" started out as slang for a particular way of talking, especially among African Americans. It later came to mean talking rhythmically over musical accompaniment. Modern rap artists draw from many sources, including the blues and spoken word poets.

The first rap performers were actually Jamaican toasters, the name for the emcees (Master of Ceremonies) at parties. Caribbean immigrants brought toasting to New York City's South Bronx. It was not long before kids in this neighborhood developed hip-hop culture, expressing themselves through graffiti art, break dancing, and rapping over tracks played and mixed by DJs. In 1979, the Sugarhill Gang introduced the terms "rap" and "hip-hop" to a global audience. Influential acts such as DJ Grandmaster Flash and the groups Run-DMC and Public Enemy pioneered the beats, lyrics, and rhymes that helped pave the way for upcoming stars including Dr. Dre, Snoop Dogg, Jay-Z, Missy Elliott, and Eminem.

In the world of modern hip-hop, Jay-Z is one of its biggest stars. Born Shawn Carter in 1969 in Brooklyn, New York, Jay-Z wrote songs about his life, and was influenced by soul artists like Marvin Gaye. He went on to win 22 Grammy awards and was the first rapper inducted into the Songwriters Hall of Fame.

BREAK DANCING

Jay-Z was president of the hip-hop record label Def Jam Recordings from 2004 to 2007.

JAY-Z

TUNEFUL**Terms**

Sampling means using a part of one song as a layer in another song. Early on, sampling meant storing snatches of sounds made by acoustic instruments on a synthesizer, and replaying those tracks at the press of a button. Later, "sampling" came to mean playing parts of existing records at the same time during DJ performances. A DJ can play short samples of one track on top of another track by using twin turntables. Favorite early hip-hop samples included James Brown's funk rhythms.

DJ SPINDERELLA MIXING BEATS USING TWIN TURNTABLES. SHE WAS A MEMBER OF THE LEGENDARY RAP GROUP SALT-N-PEPA.

 + MUSICAL MASTERS +

+ A TRIBE CALLED + QUEST

Formed in 1985 in Queens, New York, A Tribe Called Quest was a hip-hop collective featuring Q-Tip, Phife Dawg, Jarobi White, and Ali Shaheed Muhammad. In the 1990s, they were at the spearhead of a movement known as alternative hip-hop, which had a mellow, funky approach to the sounds, beats, and lyrics of hip-hop, mixing in soul and jazz. They also brought in African sounds and influences and they explored philosophy and politics in their music. Even their style was alternative, with bright colors and African-influenced patterns.

In 2016, Q-Tip was named the first Artistic Director of Hip Hop Culture at the John F. Kennedy Center for the Performing Arts.

 **LISTEN UP!**

A TRIBE CALLED QUEST, "CAN I KICK IT?"

Run-DMC
Rock The House

HIP-HOP INNOVATORS RUN-DMC (RAPPERS DARYL "DMC" MCDANIELS AND JOSEPH "REVEREND RUN" SIMMONS, together with DJ Jason "Jam Master Jay" Mizell) are shown here during a video shoot in 1984. Not afraid to back up their hip-hop with guitar rock, Run-DMC pioneered the kind of crossover artistry that today makes up most pop music. Their street-smart style and hard-hitting lyrics helped turn hip-hop into one of the most popular music styles in the world.

LYRICAL MASTER
Reverend Run raps over the beat.

SESSION MAN Eddie Martinez was a session guitarist who regularly performed with Run-DMC, especially on their "rock-rap" crossovers.

STYLE STATEMENT
The kids dancing in the audience are actors—check out their classic 1980s style, such as this oversize bow.

HATS ON Black homburg hats were another part of Run-DMC's signature look.

MEN IN BLACK Black leather was part of Run-DMC's signature look, making them grittier and more down-to-earth than many other rappers at the time, who wore flashy costumes and bright colors.

RAP LEGEND Rapper DMC strikes a pose.

CROSSOVER COVER Two years after this video was shot, Run-DMC would have their biggest hit with a rock-rap cover that featured Aerosmith themselves. The success of this record helped rap cross over into the mainstream.

Stadium **Superstars**

WHAT BETTER WAY IS THERE TO LOSE YOURSELF IN THE MUSIC than when you're surrounded by tens of thousands of screaming fans being blasted with high-volume sound from colossal speakers? In the 1980s, millions of music fans went to see their favorite rock and pop acts packing huge sports arenas. U2, Cher, and Bon Jovi got whole stadiums jumping, and today, artists including Coldplay, Ed Sheeran, and Adele continue to sell out massive venues.

Today, most people listen to music via streaming. This means that artists do not make as much money from selling their records as they used to, so they play live more often as a way to sustain their careers. But even back in the 1970s, some bands were making hundreds of millions of dollars with huge tours in massive stadiums all across the globe. The Rolling Stones have been filling stadiums for five decades and are still touring today. In the 1980s, acts such as Queen, Elton John, and Tina Turner became famous for their energetic stage shows.

The Irish rock band U2 have been filling arenas since the mid-1980s. Bono's heartfelt vocals combine with the Edge's soaring guitar solos and a powerful rhythm section to create music that is perfect for stadium shows.

Some modern solo artists like Adele and Ed Sheeran have also played large stadium acts. British singer-songwriter Ed Sheeran performs to massive sold-out crowds, often with just a guitar, loop pedal, and vocals. Featuring Sheeran's sweet, catchy pop songs, his 2018 "Divide" global tour earned more money than any other artist in 30 years, according to a research group.

Before the band landed on the name U2, they tried out the Larry Mullen Band, the Hype, and Feedback.

ED SHEERAN

U2 IN CONCERT

+ ELTON JOHN +

Reginald Kenneth Dwight grew up just outside of London and could play the piano by the age of three. He studied classical piano, but he loved blues and rock and roll. He soon changed his name to the more stage-friendly Elton Hercules John. John had dozens of hits in the 1970s with his songwriting partner Bernie Taupin, and he made sure no one ever forgot him by wearing elaborate costumes and performing hit songs at stadium-rocking concerts.

LISTEN UP!
BON JOVI, "LIVIN' ON A PRAYER"

More than 1.5 billion people from around the world watched the Live Aid concert broadcast on TV.

[BEHIND the Notes]

In 1985, British rock stars Bob Geldof and Midge Ure organized a pair of concerts to raise money to help Ethiopians who were suffering from famine. Live Aid was held on July 13th at Wembley Stadium in London, in front of 72,000 people, and at John F. Kennedy Stadium in Philadelphia, in front of 100,000 people. Many of the biggest acts in music performed, including U2, Tina Turner, David Bowie, Madonna, and Run-DMC. Queen's performance was later voted the greatest live show in the history of rock.

LIVE AID ORGANIZER BOB GELDOF WAVES TO THE CROWD AT WEMBLEY.

+ ADELE +

Adele Adkins is a British singer-songwriter who has a stadium-filling voice with an astonishing range. She's scored huge hits with deeply personal songs about love and heartbreak. Her fans also love her down-to-earth style. Adele had her first hit when she was just 20 years old, and most of her albums are named for the age she was when she wrote them. She's won an astonishing 15 Grammy Awards and has been named one of the most influential people in the world by *Time* magazine.

All In on **Afropop**

THROUGHOUT THE SECOND HALF OF THE 20TH CENTURY,
Western pop had a big effect on African popular music. Traditional African styles were mixed with Western styles and played with Western and African instruments, giving rise to more than 50 types of African pop. All of this amazing new music, known as Afropop, exploded onto the international music scene in the 1980s. It created huge international stars such as Youssou N'Dour, Mory Kanté, and Salif Keita.

YOUSSOU N'DOUR

Afropop's sounds came from many African countries, and included highlife from Ghana, mbaqanga from South Africa, juju and Afrobeat from Nigeria, *jit* from Zimbabwe, and *mbalax* from Senegal. In the 1920s, highlife was performed by brass bands. A later form of highlife, mixing in instruments such as the guitar, was one of the first Afropop styles to make a splash in the West in the 1970s. Fela Kuti blended highlife with funk to create Afrobeat (see p. 131). In Cameroon, highlife with a steady rhythm became *makossa*.

In South Africa, the Zulu township music called mbaqanga had a lilting style with a driving rhythm. You can hear this in Solomon Linda's 1939 song "Mbube," on which "The Lion Sleeps Tonight" is based. The trumpeter Hugh Masekela and his wife, Miriam Makeba, mixed mbaqanga with jazz during the 1950s and '60s. In the 1970s in Senegal, Afro-Cuban music mixed with local sabar drum rhythms to create mbalax. The most famous mbalax singer is Youssou N'Dour. Zimbabwe's jit music is dance music with a strong drumbeat that combines traditional Shona melodies with rhythm and blues on the guitar.

THE GHANAIAN HIGHLIFE BAND OSIBISA BECAME FAMOUS IN THE 1970s.

+ MUSICAL MASTER +

+ SALIF KEITA +

Salif Keita is a renowned Afropop musician from Mali in West Africa. He was born albino, with pale skin, eyes, and hair, which is rare for Africans. Despite facing threats for his skin condition, Keita was determined to make music. His band Les Ambassadeurs was a worldwide success, mixing local traditional mandingo music with Afro-Cuban and soul styles. Keita has recorded with the Mexican-American musician Carlos Santana, and he was the first African bandleader to receive a Grammy Award nomination.

Salif Keita's soulful sound has earned him the title the "Golden Voice of Africa."

 **LISTEN UP!**

KING SUNNY ADÉ, "JA FUNMI"

+ AWESOME INSTRUMENT +
NGONI

THE NGONI IS A WOODEN STRING INSTRUMENT FROM WEST AFRICA, **and** it is played by the griots, traditional musical storytellers who passed their craft down through the generations. A ngoni has a hollowed-out body with dried animal skin stretched over it, a narrow neck, and it usually has four strings. Bassekou Kouyaté is a ngoni master from Mali who broke tradition by playing ngoni standing up. His band, Ngoni Ba, featured ngoni instead of guitars.

NGONI ➤

Some historians think that banjos evolved from ngonis that were brought to North America by enslaved West Africans.

KING SUNNY ADÉ

[TUNEFUL **Terms**]

Juju is an Afropop style based on the traditional music of the Yoruba people from southwest Nigeria. It combines singing and poetry with drumming, especially the talking drum. This drum is shaped like an hourglass and can be squeezed to change the pitch, which makes it sound like the instrument is talking. Electric guitars and keyboards are played alongside the talking drum. The best known juju star is King Sunny Adé, also known as the "King of Juju" and "Minister of Enjoyment."

159

Less Is **More**

MINIMALISM IS A MUSIC STYLE THAT USES JUST A FEW SIMPLE SOUNDS, such as repeated drum beats or electronic notes that change slightly and build into complicated patterns. Minimalism may seem easy to compose and play, but it's really difficult to do it well. The first minimalist composers included Americans Terry Riley and Philip Glass, who were both looking for ways to change classical music. The style spread into pop music through the German band Kraftwerk, who ended up inspiring both hip-hop and electronic dance music (EDM).

When a group of American composers, including Philip Glass and Steve Reich, were looking to put their modern stamp on classical music in the 1960s, they began experimenting with using simple sounds—for example, a person saying a few words or notes played on a synthesizer. They applied new techniques to the sounds, including looping, which links the end of a track to its beginning so that it plays in a continuous loop. Because the music is made with the bare minimum of sources, it's known as minimalism.

In the mid-1970s, minimalism inspired the musician Brian Eno from the band Roxy Music to produce gentle, atmospheric music that is sometimes called ambient. At the same time, the influential German pop band Kraftwerk used electronic sounds to create minimalist music played over drum machine beats. Hip-hop pioneers in the early 1980s happily sampled from Kraftwerk's tracks. The band also inspired DJs who made EDM.

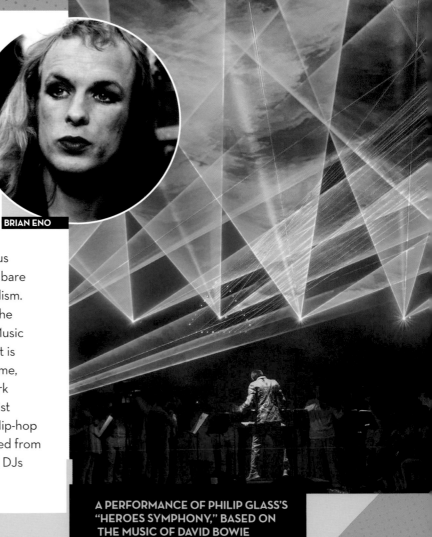

BRIAN ENO

A PERFORMANCE OF PHILIP GLASS'S "HEROES SYMPHONY," BASED ON THE MUSIC OF DAVID BOWIE

+ MUSICAL MASTERS +

+ KRAFTWERK +

Still playing today, Kraftwerk is a German electronic pop group led by Ralf Hütter. In 1968, Hütter and Florian Schneider began experimenting with synthesizers, trying to combine classical music with American pop. Their breakout success came with the album *Autobahn* in 1974. The group also helped create techno with their 1977 record *Trans-Europa Express*. Countless pop bands, including Depeche Mode, New Order, and Daft Punk, have been inspired by Kraftwerk's music.

When Kraftwerk performs the song "The Robots," the band is replaced by four robots that move to the music.

+ AWESOME INSTRUMENT +
DRUM MACHINE

THE DRUM MACHINE HAS PLAYED A KEY PART IN POP SINCE THE 1980s. A type of synthesizer, it copies—or samples—drum sounds and plays them in perfect, unending rhythm. In 1980, the relatively affordable and easy to use Roland TR-808 drum machine made its debut. Suddenly, anyone with access to the 808 could produce all kinds of electronic music, whether in a recording studio or at home in their basement.

ROLAND TR-808 ▼

LISTEN UP!
PHILIP GLASS, "MAD RUSH"

Afrika Bambaataa used a Roland TR-808 to create the funky beat of the early hip-hop hit "Planet Rock" in 1982.

Dance to the Music

ELECTRONIC DANCE MUSIC (OR EDM) FIRST APPEARED ON THE CLUB SCENES IN THE 1970s in Chicago and New York, when DJs started mixing different styles of music, including Jamaican dub and minimalist electropop. They wanted to create a sound that was entirely focused on dancing, making rhythms that continued from one track to the next. These days, there are a huge variety of EDM styles, from house to techno to garage—and the dancing has never stopped.

Nigerian DJ Obi set a world record by DJing for 240 hours in 2016.

DJ DAVID GUETTA COLLABORATES WITH POP, RAP, AND SOUL STARS AS WELL AS EDM ARTISTS SUCH AS DJ KRYOMAN, PICTURED HERE IN HIS ROBOT SUIT EQUIPPED WITH LED LIGHTS.

House music probably takes its name from the Warehouse, a dance club in Chicago that happened to have some highly creative DJs, such as Frankie Knuckles, in the late 1970s. At about the same time, New York DJ Larry Levan was creating a similar style, but his club was called the Paradise Garage—which is where garage music started. These experimental DJs played with techniques, drum machines, and other electronic equipment to turn existing tracks into their own new music. They took inspiration from all over the place, especially Jamaican DJs and the German band Kraftwerk.

In the 1980s, as house and garage spread around the world, techno developed, too. Techno is simple dance music that uses mostly drum tracks and a few electronic sounds. The style influenced mainstream artists from Madonna to Depeche Mode. The never-ending dance party continued as other international acts created more new styles, including ambient house and trance. By the end of the 20th century, EDM was beginning to be considered part of mainstream music.

FRANKIE KNUCKLES

+ AWESOME INSTRUMENT +
DAW

THE KEY PIECE OF EQUIPMENT FOR CREATING EDM IS A DIGITAL AUDIO WORKSTATION (DAW). It is sometimes known as a studio in a box, and it brings together the technology and software needed to create, record, edit, mix, change, and play sounds. It can create everything from movie soundtracks to dance music. Modern DAWs use sound editing computer programs such as ProTools and Cubase; they have special sound-processing microchips and often a synthesizer.

IN 1993, MOBY (BELOW) RELEASED "THOUSAND," THE FASTEST SINGLE IN HISTORY. IT PEAKED AT 1,015 BPM.

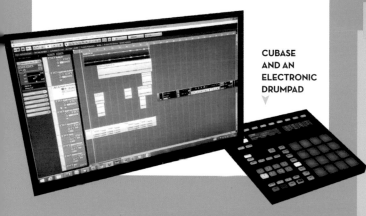

CUBASE AND AN ELECTRONIC DRUMPAD

[BEHIND the Notes]

The rhythm of a track tells you how many beats are played in each bar or measure, but it does not tell you how fast they are played. This is decided by the track's tempo, and one way to measure tempo is in beats per minute (bpm). Each type of music has a particular bpm. Reggae usually has 60–90 bpm; hip-hop has 60–100 bpm; jazz, funk, and disco have about 120 bpm; and techno has 120–140 bpm.

The world's slowest musical performance, by a German church organ, is due to finish in 2640!

🔊 LISTEN UP!
DAFT PUNK, "ONE MORE TIME"

★ **+ MUSICAL MASTERS +**

+ DAFT PUNK +

Daft Punk is a French EDM duo known for playing a blend of house, funk, techno, and electronic pop mixed with everything from disco to hard rock. Guy-Manuel de Homem-Christo and Thomas Bangalter started out playing indie rock, but they discovered EDM in the 1990s and now wear robot costumes and helmets when they perform. Daft Punk has worked with other musicians, such as Pharrell Williams, and the band wrote the score for the 2011 movie *Tron: Legacy*.

SOME OF THE BIGGEST NAMES IN POPULAR MUSIC brought the genre to the next level with elaborate stage performances and music videos, and chart-topping hits and albums. Here are some musicians who broke records, had legions of fans, created instantly recognizable tracks, and made their own important contributions to pop culture and music history.

MICHAEL JACKSON

1958–2009

Michael Jackson, who was also known as the "King of Pop," was the biggest pop star in history. Jackson's career started at age 11, when he scored a No. 1 hit with four of his brothers in their band, the Jackson 5. His 1982 solo album *Thriller* became the second biggest-selling record of all time. An astonishing performer, Jackson created dance moves, such as the backward-gliding moonwalk. His exciting and energetic music videos were the first by a black artist to be shown regularly on television.

DOLLY PARTON

b. 1946

Dolly Parton was the fourth of 12 children growing up in Tennessee's Smoky Mountains. Parton's family was musical, and she would become one of the greatest singer-songwriters in the history of country music. By the age of 13, she had performed on the *Grand Ole Opry* country show. Her breakthrough hit "Dumb Blonde" came in 1967. While Dolly often played a simple and silly character onstage, in reality she is a supersmart businesswoman, a talented actress, and one of the great American songwriters.

BRITNEY SPEARS

b. 1981

Teen sensation Britney Spears began her career as a cast member of *The All New Mickey Mouse Club*. At the age of 17, she burst onto the pop scene with the single "Baby, One More Time," and her album of the same name entered the *Billboard* charts at No. 1. Three albums followed soon after, propelling Spears to global stardom. Over a two-decade career with nine album releases, she has sold 100 million records worldwide and has received numerous awards, including a Grammy.

RED HOT CHILI PEPPERS

Formed 1983

Groundbreaking Californian band Red Hot Chili Peppers have blended funk, punk rock, and rap to create an entirely new sound. With their edgy outfits and exciting stage antics, they have also built a reputation as one of rock's best live acts. The original band was formed by four school friends. Its lineup has undergone many changes over the years, although lead vocalist Anthony Kiedis and bassist Flea (Michael Balzary) have remained constants. With more than 80 million records sold worldwide, and three Grammy Awards, they are one of the best-selling bands of all time.

GLORIA ESTEFAN

b. 1957

Gloria Estefan overcame life-changing injuries, became an advocate for political freedoms, and is one of the biggest Latin pop stars to achieve crossover success. When she was a baby, Gloria's parents fled to Miami from dictators in Cuba. Throughout the 1980s, her band Miami Sound Machine had hits including "Conga" and "Rhythm is Gonna Get You." In 1990, Gloria's tour bus was hit by a truck, breaking her spine. She recovered with the help of surgically implanted metal pins and still makes music today.

Rockin' Country

COUNTRY IS A VARIED MUSIC CATEGORY THESE DAYS, and some of its most famous singers are crossover country pop stars, such as Carrie Underwood and Taylor Swift. The roots of country pop go back to the Nashville sound of the 1950s. Dolly Parton and Garth Brooks are among the musicians who played a part in the rise of country pop, as did country music radio stations. Today, big money can be made in country, with its greatest stars filling huge stadiums and arenas on tour.

Country music producers have long sought to make their style as popular as rock and roll. Traditional country elements, from fiddles to twangy, nasally singing, have mostly been dropped over time in a move to be more mainstream. Strong voices and musical arrangements, including string instruments and backup vocals, helped produce country stars including Patsy Cline, Tammy Wynette, and Roy Orbison in the 1960s. Country pop really took off in the 1970s with the help of musicians such as Dolly Parton and Kenny Rogers.

While some traditionalists, such as Willie Nelson and Neil Young, refused to let pop influence their music, country pop was here to stay. In the 1980s, huge audiences tuned in to country music radio shows. As grunge developed, some listeners went looking for songs that were more upbeat—and they found them on their local country stations. The popularity of Garth Brooks, who mixed mainstream rock with country in the 1990s, helped pave the way for a long list of next generation crossover successes, such as Dixie Chicks, Miranda Lambert, Kelly Clarkson, and Blake Shelton.

DIXIE CHICKS

Dixie Chicks named their band after a 1973 song called "Dixie Chicken" by Little Feat.

Emmylou Harris began her career as a folk singer; she has admitted she once looked down on country.

[TUNEFUL **Terms**]

Country rock mixes rock sounds and instruments with country themes and influences. One of the first musicians to combine the two was Gram Parsons in the late 1960s. Even Bob Dylan recorded a country rock album in 1969, called *Nashville Skyline*, with musicians that included Johnny Cash. By the 1970s, country rock was an established style, with artists including Linda Ronstadt, Emmylou Harris, and Neil Young performing it. The Eagles, who became the biggest-selling American band in history, were a California rock band with country influences.

THE COUNTRY-ROCK SINGER EMMYLOU HARRIS HAS WON 13 GRAMMY AWARDS.

LISTEN UP!
KEITH URBAN, "DAYS GO BY"

+ **MUSICAL MASTER** +

+ **KEITH URBAN** +

Country rock superstar Keith Urban was raised in Australia and made his first album in 1988. After moving to Nashville, Tennessee, in 1992, he made a splash with his band, The Ranch, playing his rowdy brand of country blended with rock guitar. In 2000, Urban launched his solo career, scoring his first No. 1 hit, "But for the Grace of God." In 2006, his marriage to actress Nicole Kidman grabbed the headlines, and his star power continued to grow. His albums have sold more than 15 million copies. In 2012, he was made a member of the Grand Ole Opry—one of country music's biggest honors.

Girl Power

IN THE 1990s AND 2000s, A FRESH WAVE OF ARTISTS brought messages of female empowerment to a new generation of kids. Inspired by earlier stars such as Madonna and Aretha, they mixed pop influences with hip-hop and other styles. Acts such as Destiny's Child, Missy Elliott, and the Spice Girls sang about the importance of making your own money, taking pride in your looks, and being independent and confident. From what they wore to the lyrics they sang, they spoke directly to their fans—both male and female.

QUEEN LATIFAH

Icons of the 1980s, such as Madonna, had blazed a trail for strong women in pop, but in many other styles of music, negative messages about women were as loud as ever. Some acts, such as Salt-N-Pepa, had stood up for women in hip-hop in the 1980s, and in the 1990s singers and producers Queen Latifah and Missy Elliott became two of the biggest names in rap—and feminist icons, too.

Girl groups showed that they had the ability to connect to younger female audiences. R&B supergroup Destiny's Child had hits with feminist anthems such as "Independent Women" and "Survivor." Band member Beyoncé Knowles went on to become one of the world's biggest pop megastars and an iconic figure. From Britain, the Spice Girls preached their own brand of feminist empowerment that they called "Girl Power." They sang about the importance of friendship and family, as well as being confident and assertive. You can hear the influence of these acts when you listen to today's girl power superstars, such as Katy Perry, Rihanna, and Ariana Grande.

SPICE GIRLS

+ MUSICAL MASTER +

+ ALICIA KEYS +

Alicia Keys is a singer, songwriter, producer, actress, activist, and business owner from New York City. Keys grew up learning classical piano and started writing her own songs at the age of 12. Her first single, "Fallin'," topped the Billboard charts in 2001, and her first album, *Songs in A Minor,* sold more than 12 million copies worldwide. Her success continued with six studio albums, and she was a coach on NBC's show *The Voice* for three seasons.

+ MUSICAL MASTER +

+ BEYONCÉ +

Beyoncé Knowles is an American performer who first became famous in Destiny's Child along with Kelly Rowland and Michelle Williams. Beyoncé recorded her first solo album in 2003 and is one of the world's biggest stars, known for celebrating female power, especially in her 2013 album *Beyoncé.* She has also starred in movies, including *Dreamgirls* (2006), in which she played a character loosely based on the singer Diana Ross. Beyoncé is married to rapper Jay-Z, and together, they have toured around the world.

> In 2019, Missy Elliott became the first female rapper inducted to the Songwriters Hall of Fame.

+ MUSICAL MASTER +

+ MISSY ELLIOTT +

Melissa "Misdemeanor" Elliott, aka Missy Elliott, is a rapper, songwriter, producer, and actor from Virginia, U.S.A. She had a difficult childhood, and she credits her mother with showing her the meaning of true strength. She started off in an all-female R&B group and worked in a writing and producing team with her friend Timbaland, before launching her solo career in 1997. Her 2002 album is the biggest-selling album ever by a female hip-hop artist.

🔊 LISTEN UP!
BEYONCÉ, "IRREPLACEABLE"

> At the age of seven, Beyoncé won her first talent show by singing a cover of "Imagine," by John Lennon.

169

Let's hear it for **Boy Bands!**

WHEN THE BOY BAND ONE DIRECTION ANNOUNCED THEY WOULD BE TAKING A BREAK IN 2016, hearts broke around the world. With their sweet voices and highly choreographed dance routines, boy bands are designed to capture the tween and teen girl market. But the boy bands that have topped the charts in the late 2000s, including the Jonas Brothers, JLS, and 5 Seconds to Summer, have roots that go back to the early days of popular music. The classic elements of boy bands were established back in the 1960s.

The barbershop quartet, a group of men singing a capella, or unaccompanied, was perhaps the earliest version of the boy band. But it was the Beatlemania of the mid-1960s that showed just how excited fans could get about young male musicians with matching outfits and haircuts. Copycat acts sprang up everywhere. The Monkees had their own TV show, Motown signed the Jackson 5, and Menudo became the biggest Latin boy band in history.

Then came New Edition in 1983, who sang in an R&B style, and New Kids on the Block, who breathed new life into the teen pop scene and set the template for later bands. Perhaps the 1990s and early 2000s was the true boy band era, when the sounds of Take That, *NSYNC, Backstreet Boys, and Boyz II Men dominated the charts. In the 2010s, the success of boy bands such as One Direction encouraged a resurgence of boy band mania. The Backstreet Boys re-formed, and Take That are still thrilling fans with their shows as a three-piece group.

The Jackson 5 were the first band to have four straight No. 1s on the *Billboard* charts.

JACKSON 5

ONE DIRECTION

170

+ MUSICAL MASTERS +

+ *NSYNC +

*NSYNC was an American boy band with members Justin Timberlake, JC Chasez, Chris Kirkpatrick, Joey Fatone, and Lance Bass. The group performed hits like "Bye Bye Bye" in the mid-90s and early 2000s. The band split up in 2002, due in part to Justin Timberlake's solo career. Timberlake's first solo album earned the number two spot on the *Billboard* 200 chart, and he went on to star in several movies. He even recorded the original song "Can't Stop the Feeling!" for the 2016 movie *Trolls*.

+ MUSICAL MASTERS +

+ JONAS BROTHERS +

Brothers Nick, Joe, and Kevin rocketed to fame after signing a deal with Disney's Hollywood Records and appearing on the Disney Channel. The trio had been around for a while, but their appearances in Disney movies such as *Camp Rock* and in their own reality TV series gained them a huge following. The brothers released five albums, selling more than eight million copies worldwide. The band's unexpected split in 2012 came as a bombshell to their adoring fans, but they started performing together again in 2019.

[TUNEFUL Terms]

A cappella means "in the style of the church." Instruments may have been forbidden in early church music so people sang unaccompanied. A cappella singing became popular in North America from 1895 to 1930, thanks to the success of barbershop quartets, and then the popularity of doo-wop street corner singers. Today's "manufactured" boy bands are, of course, required to have good vocals, but the members don't always play their own instruments. Boy bands tend to use good looks, a stage presence, and slick dance moves to gain fans and sell tickets.

LISTEN UP!
ONE DIRECTION,
"WHAT MAKES YOU BEAUTIFUL"

In the TV show *Glee*, the Dalton Academy Warblers are a fictional a cappella group from a private school in Ohio, U.S.A.

They've Got
Talent!

SINCE THE AMERICAN BOY BAND O-TOWN WERE CREATED FOR SEASON ONE OF MTV'S *MAKING THE BAND* IN 2000, talent shows such as the *The Voice*, *American Idol*, and *K-Pop Star* have given a start to a number of huge acts, including One Direction (who only came in third in their talent show), Jennifer Hudson, Carrie Underwood, and Kelly Clarkson. Talent shows give artists a chance to build up a big fan base in a short time, thanks to massive TV and online exposure.

FINAL FAREWELL
This performance, at the Dolby Theater in Hollywood, California, in April 2016, was part of the "Farewell" season of the hit TV series *American Idol* before the show moved to ABC for the 2017–2018 season.

WITH THE BAND Talent shows use experienced musicians to back up the contestants.

FUTURE STAR? Maybe someone in this audience could be a contestant in the next hit TV talent show—could they end up being a star?

CHRIS DAUGHTRY

JAMES DURBIN

SPECTACULAR SHOW
A talent show such as *American Idol* gives new artists a chance to put on a show at a scale normally reserved for huge stars.

ONE-HIT WONDERS?
Winning performers are usually guaranteed at least one hit record, but only a few go on to enjoy lasting pop careers.

CALEB JOHNSON

CONSTANTINE MAROULIS

JUDGE AND JURY The judges are a vital part of any talent show. Often, there will be a "mean" one that viewers love to hate.

MUSICAL MENTORS Many talent shows have judges who take on and mentor the competing acts. This helps to create a story for the series and builds excitement.

Cue Up the **K-pop**

A KEY PART OF KOREA'S CULTURE SINCE 1992, Korean pop music, or K-pop, is finding audiences across the globe. The music is known for its catchy tunes, and for the way tribes of fans devote themselves to their favorite performers. K-pop is a highly orchestrated industry, with especially young musicians being auditioned and fed into a training system that produces stars. They practice for years to perfect their K-pop personas.

Throughout the 1980s, most Korean pop songs were soft, syrupy ballads. But everything changed in April 1992, when the group Seo Taiji and Boys appeared on a televised talent competition. They performed a song that was a mash-up of hip-hop, synth pop, and a rhythm and blues style called new jack swing. The band got a low score from the judges, but audiences went wild for their sound and look, and a musical revolution began.

In the 1990s, three studios began producing a series of huge K-pop acts, creating what is known as the idol system. The studios train thousands of carefully selected young performers to sing, dance, and pull off complicated routines. The first K-pop product of the idol system was the boy band H.O.T. in 1996. After a slump in popularity in the early 2000s, today K-pop is firmly back in business with worldwide acts such as BTS, Blackpink, EXO, Seventeen, NCT, and Stray Kids winning millions of fans. Boyband BTS, in particular, are hugely popular and have been propelled by an enormous online and social media presence.

BTS are also known as Bangtan Boys or Bulletproof Boy Scouts.

BTS'S MIX OF HIP-HOP, POP, AND R&B HAS MADE THEM GLOBAL STARS.

+ MUSICAL MASTER +

+ PSY +

Park Jae-sang is a Korean rapper known as Psy, and he became a worldwide phenomenon when the video for his 2012 song, "Gangnam Style," about a neighborhood in Seoul, Korea, became a record-breaking hit online. Psy immediately became the face of K-pop, despite the fact that he looks and acts nothing like a traditional K-pop idol. "Gangnam Style" became the most successful Asian music hit ever.

[TUNEFUL **Terms**]

J-pop is Japanese pop—it is similar to K-pop and inspired the Korean version. J-pop studios tightly control carefully produced acts, such as Morning Musume (a girl band with a changing roster of members) or the Johnnys, which is the term for the young and attractive boy bands created by super-producer Johnny Kitagawa. J-pop features upbeat bubblegum pop and love songs. TV appearances and merchandise sales matter just as much as the music.

LISTEN UP!
GIRLS' GENERATION, "GEE"

[BEHIND **the Notes**]

With more than one billion online views, Psy's "Gangnam Style" ignited a worldwide craze for catchy K-pop dance routines and iconic moves. Big Bang's wiper dance from the song "Fantastic Baby," Super Junior's "Sorry Sorry," and the hit "I Am the Best" by 2NE1 all feature famous steps for fans to copy in front of their bedroom mirror.

SINCE 1997, MORE THAN 40 SINGERS HAVE PERFORMED WITH J-POP BAND MORNING MUSUME.

BIG BANG

Big Bang has sold over 140 million albums— more than the Jackson 5 and Backstreet Boys.

175

Breaking the Mold

GENRE-HOPPING IS NOTHING NEW IN MUSIC. The Beatles played pop, hard rock, and blues in the 1960s. In the following decade, David Bowie dipped into folk, glam rock, soul, and electronic music. Many performers in the 21st century, such as Ed Sheeran, The 1975, Lana Del Rey, and THEY., are difficult to fit into a category and have been praised for their ability to produce different sounds. Even Justin Bieber, Miley Cyrus, and The Weeknd could argue their music does not conform to a genre.

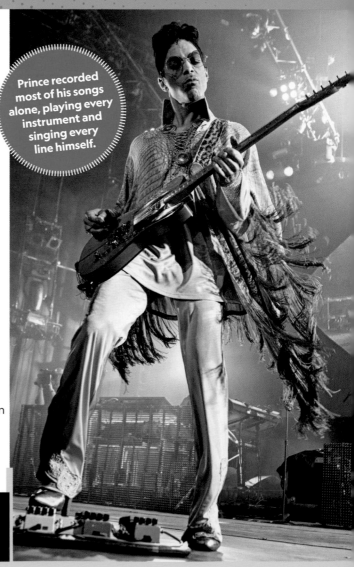

Prince recorded most of his songs alone, playing every instrument and singing every line himself.

Childish Gambino (the recording name of singer-songwriter, DJ, actor, and comedian Donald Glover) said in 2017, "I think genre is dead ... There really is no genre anymore, so you just have to make something new." The music he makes fuses many styles, including funk, hip-hop, and '70s-style rock. In one of his hit singles you can hear the influence of one of the most prolific genre-hopping artists in history—Prince. This singer, songwriter, producer, and multi-instrumentalist mastered every style of music he turned to across a career that began in the late 1970s and lasted for nearly four decades.

Some of the biggest hits of the 21st century have not followed any particular type of music, and many of today's top artists, including Bruno Mars, Lady Gaga, and Rihanna, leapfrog in and out of styles. Canadian rapper Drake became a star by mixing hip-hop with rhythm and blues, and his 2017 album includes the flavors of Caribbean dancehall, Afrobeat, English grime, and a style of hip-hop called trap.

CHILDISH GAMBINO

MODERN-DAY VIRTUOSO PRINCE PLAYED GUITAR, KEYBOARDS, AND DRUMS.

Taylor Swift grew up on a Christmas tree farm in Reading, Pennsylvania, U.S.A.

★ + MUSICAL MASTER +

+ TAYLOR SWIFT +

Taylor Swift was already a country music singer by her early teens, but her ability to create fresh sounds and commercial hits has seen her become a megastar across many genres. After the incredible success of her first album, *Taylor Swift*, the songs on *Fearless* reached fans of pop, soft rock, and folk as well as her country-base followers. Swift's biggest hit, "Shake It Off," was released in 2014 and is a funky dance song with no guitars. She is as comfortable creating a pure pop tune as she is a song that will storm the Country Music Association (CMA) Awards.

🔊 LISTEN UP!
PHARRELL WILLIAMS, "HAPPY"

[BEHIND the Notes]

Since 1959, the Recording Academy (formerly the American National Academy of Recording Arts and Sciences) has presented annual awards known as the Grammys (Gramophone Awards). Originally there were 23 categories of music that received awards, but today there are 83. The most coveted Grammy Awards are Album of the Year, Record of the Year, Song of the Year, and Best New Artist. The actual trophy given to a Grammy Award winner is a small, gold copy of an old-fashioned gramophone.

In 2014, Bruno Mars donated $100,000 to the victims of a typhoon in the Philippines.

BRUNO MARS, WHOSE MUSIC BLENDS HIP-HOP, SOUL, FUNK, AND ROCK, CELEBRATES A GRAMMY WIN.

177

Full Stream **Ahead**

ARE YOU STREAMING MUSIC WHILE YOU READ THIS?

Technology has been changing the world of music since prehistoric times, and these days are no different. Most people don't buy much recorded music anymore, choosing instead to stream tracks on a phone or tablet. No doubt, the digital age has affected what we listen to and how we hear it. But what do those changes mean for the artists who make music?

The internet makes it possible for almost anyone, anywhere to listen to almost any music that has ever been recorded. And the music industry is struggling to cope with that. Since the 2000s, it's been easy for anyone online to download digital audio files (normally in mp3 format) without paying for them. More recently, legal streaming sites such as Spotify have gained popularity. Whether it's a pirated downloaded file or a streaming playlist, many people don't spend money on recordings anymore (though some believe old-school traditional vinyl records are still the best way to listen to music).

Musicians and the music industry have responded in different ways. Big record labels have tried to make money from streaming services, while musicians earn their keep by touring and doing more live performances. The good news is that the internet, social media, and audio technology such as DAWs (see p. 165) have actually made it much easier for more artists to make music and find an audience without following the traditional route of signing with a record label.

WITH OVER 8.2 BILLION STREAMS, DRAKE WAS SPOTIFY'S MOST STREAMED ARTIST IN 2018.

SPOTIFY

ARIANA GRANDE'S 2019 ALBUM _THANK U, NEXT_ SET A RECORD WITH 307 MILLION STREAMS IN ITS FIRST WEEK.

BEHIND the Notes

Social media makes it easy to spread ideas quickly, whether they are dance moves, songs, or videos. Online hits have become important to the music business, because viral crazes taken from music videos or songs can help to sell tracks and create artist buzz. Canadian chart topper Shawn Mendes used a short video-sharing app to promote his songs and lyrics, which led to him being signed by Island Records. Justin Bieber, Austin Mahone, and Charlie Puth can all credit their breakthroughs to the power of online videos.

SHAWN MENDES BECAME FAMOUS FOR HIS SIX-SECOND VIDEO SNIPPETS ONLINE.

+ MUSICAL MASTER +

+ LADY GAGA +

Lady Gaga is a master of social media, with around 180 million online fans and followers. Born Stefani Germanotta in 1986, she burst onto the pop scene in 2008 with huge hits such as "Poker Face." Since then, her albums have explored rock, EDM, jazz, and techno-pop, while her dazzling and provocative outfits have set the internet ablaze. She's an Oscar-winning actress and a passionate activist, too, using social media to support social and political causes.

🔊 **LISTEN UP!**

LADY GAGA, "BORN THIS WAY"

BEHIND the Notes

Even in the digital age, the experience of seeing a live act is still the ultimate way to connect to a favorite singer or band. Nowadays, music lovers in the United States can choose from hundreds of festivals and gigs. From multiday events featuring popular singers like Katy Perry and Beyoncé, at high-profile events such as Coachella, Lollapalooza, and Austin City Limits to more laid-back gatherings at the Blue Ox and Nelsonville, there's a festival for every type of fan.

KATY PERRY AT THE KAABOO FESTIVAL

At the age of 15, Katy Perry released a gospel album under the name Katy Hudson.

179

THANKS TO TECHNOLOGY AND CONNECTIVITY AROUND THE GLOBE, 21st-century music will continue to develop, change, and diversify. Artists who once might have been known only in a small corner of the world can now promote their way to international stardom. Unique musicians playing unusual styles can make their music easy to find online. If they want to stay fresh in their fan base's eyes, today's stars have to think globally when it comes to music, touring, and platforms.

JANELLE MONÁE

b. 1985

A savvy businesswoman, an experimental artist with dazzling sci-fi vision, a movie star, a feminist activist, and a pop sensation: Janelle Monáe is all of these and more. Much of her work explores a futuristic world in which she is an android called Cindi Mayweather. As well as making hit records, she has starred in Oscar-nominated movies, including *Hidden Figures*. Monáe is also famous for refusing to follow gender norms in her life and work, and especially in her distinctive personal style, such as her trademark tuxedo.

RIHANNA

b. 1988

The most successful recording artist of the digital era, Robyn Rihanna Fenty left the Caribbean island of Barbados to conquer the world. Her career got a jump-start when vacationing record execs heard her sing. Since then, she has become an R&B powerhouse, releasing some of the biggest hits of all time, including "Umbrella" and "We Found Love." Rihanna is also a movie star, a successful businesswoman, and a humanitarian who speaks out to give kids around the world the right to decent education and health care.

KENDRICK LAMAR

b. 1987

Kendrick Lamar Duckworth grew up in Compton, a neighborhood of Los Angeles, California. He is famous for his complex rap lyrics that tell stories and paint pictures with words. His breakthrough album was released in 2012, and spent 300 weeks on the Billboard 200 charts, making him the second rapper in history to accomplish such a feat. His fourth album, released in 2017, won several Grammy Awards and the Pulitzer Prize for Music, which had never before been given to a hip-hop artist.

BRUNO MARS

b. 1985

When Peter Hernandez was only four years old, he was performing as the youngest Elvis impersonator in Hawaii and had been given the nickname "Bruno." He was part of his family's music show, and he later impersonated Michael Jackson's singing and moves. In 2003, he moved to California to break into the music industry and started writing songs for other people. Then, in 2010, he became a star pop performer as Bruno Mars. In 2015, he had a massive hit with "Uptown Funk," which he cowrote with Mark Ronson. Mars has also starred in two Super Bowl halftime shows.

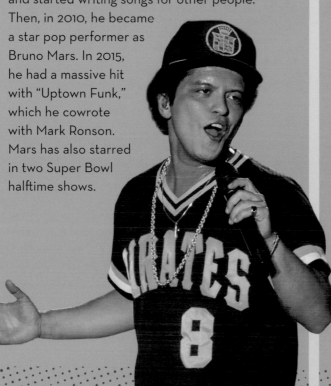

IMAGINE DRAGONS

Formed 2008

From Las Vegas, Nevada, U.S.A., rock group Imagine Dragons has rocketed to global success with a series of hits featuring crashing drums, powerful lyrics, and gripping musical hooks. Songs such as "Radioactive" and "Believer" are the kind of track you play to pump yourself up for a big game or crucial exam. Group front man Dan Reynolds has a special focus on supporting young people to be accepted for who they are so that everyone can experience love and support.

Timeline

THIS TIMELINE SHOWS ALL OF MUSIC HISTORY. We had to fold it up to fit it all in, and because more things have happened in the last few hundred years than most of the rest of musical history put together, more recent times get more space in the timeline, while the distant past is squeezed into a smaller space.

40,000 years ago Oldest surviving carved musical instruments are made

ca. 2500 B.C. Lyres are played in ancient Ur (now in Iraq)

ca. 1390 B.C. Musicians and dancers are painted on the walls of the ancient Egyptian tomb of Nebamun

ca. 1000 B.C. Samaveda hymns of ancient India are composed, one of the sources of Indian classical music

ca. 550 B.C. Ancient Greek mathematician Pythagoras notices a connection between the length of a string and the notes sounded by plucking it

ca. 100 B.C. Ancient Romans borrow from the Greeks a system for playing music, called modes

ca. A.D. 600 European monks start singing plainsong

1603 Izumo no Okuni invents kabuki theatre in Japan

1723 Vivaldi composes *The Four Seasons*

ca. 1750 Start of the Classical era of classical music

BEIJING OPERA

1790 Beijing opera is created in China

1791 Mozart's opera *The Magic Flute* opens

ca. 1810 The start of the Romantic era of classical music

1827 Beethoven's Symphony No.5 debuts

1871 The Fisk Jubilee Singers make spirituals popular in the U.S. and Europe

1876 Wagner's *Ring Cycle* operas are first performed

1956 Elvis Presley has three hit records in a row

1959 Berry Gordy starts Motown Records in Detroit

1961 Bob Dylan arrives in New York and starts singing in cafes

1964 The Beatles tour America; the start of the British Invasion

1968 The first funk record is released by James Brown: *Say It Loud: I'm Black and I'm Proud*

1968 The birth of reggae music in Jamaica

1970 The *Soul Train* music show starts broadcasting

1970 The birth of heavy metal

1975 The birth of punk rock

1979 The Sugarhill Gang makes rap and hip-hop famous

EDDIE VAN HALEN

GUIDO D'AREZZO

A TROBAIRITZ

ca. A.D. 620 Bilal ibn Rabah becomes the first muezzin

ca. A.D. 700 Medieval Indian Hindu musicians start playing zithers

ca. A.D. 900 Europeans start using polyphony (singing more than one melody at a time)

ca. A.D. 1000 Italian monk Guido d'Arezzo starts writing down music in a form called notation

ca. 1200 Troubadours and trobairitz (male and female musicians and singers) write songs in the castles of medieval France

ca. 1400 Aztec start playing huehuetl and teponaztli drums

ca. 1550 Mian Tansen creates the classics of Hindu music

1597 First European opera is composed

ca. 1600 The beginning of the Baroque era of Western classical music

ca. 1900 The birth of jazz in New Orleans

1903 W. C. Handy first hears blues music in the Mississippi Delta region of the U.S.

1925 First broadcast of the *Grand Ole Opry* radio show

1927 Duke Ellington's big band starts playing at the Cotton Club in New York

1935 Benny Goodman makes swing popular

ca. 1942 Charlie Parker and fellow musicians create bebop jazz

1943 *Oklahoma!* opens on Broadway in New York

1947 Lata Mangeshkar starts working in the Bollywood film industry as a playback singer

ca. 1979 DJs at clubs in New York and Chicago create EDM

1982 Michael Jackson releases the second biggest-selling album of all time, *Thriller*

1985 Live Aid concerts

1992 The birth of K-pop

2002 *American Idol* begins

2003 Beyoncé goes solo

2012 Psy's music video for the song "Gangnam Style" goes viral online.

2016 David Bowie releases his final album, *Blackstar*

PSY

BEYONCÉ

Glossary

Aria A long song for a solo voice, usually in an opera.

Arrange To make changes to a piece of music so that it can be played in a different way, for example by a particular instrument.

Bass Bass notes are the lowest-sounding notes in a piece of music. Bass is also the name for the lowest vocal range.

Bebop A type of jazz music from the 1940s with complex harmonies and rhythms.

Bhangra An upbeat style of folk music originating from the Punjab region of the Indian subcontinent.

Bow A curved rod with horsehair stretched along it, used to play a stringed instrument.

Call-and-response Music in which a first (often solo) part is answered by a second (often ensemble) part.

Chamber music Music written for a small group of musicians.

Chant A short musical passage for the voice, with two or more phrases that are often repeated.

Chord A group of three or more notes played at the same time.

Chorus The part of a song that is sung after each verse. It is usually designed to be catchy and memorable. A chorus can also be a large group of singers.

Clef A symbol at the start of a piece of music that informs the musician whether the lines on the staff are for higher or lower notes.

Composer A person who writes music.

Concerto A piece of music for a solo instrument accompanied by an orchestra.

Dancehall A style of music that developed from reggae, with strong rhythms and lyrics sung in the native Jamaican language.

Disco A style of dance music combining soul music and a regular bass beat, especially popular in the 1970s.

Dissonance Music that lacks harmony and sounds harsh and discordant.

DJ Disc jockey—a person who plays recorded music to a live audience, on the radio or in a dance club.

Electronic music Music with sounds created purely electronically by the instrument's technology.

Ensemble A small group of musicians who play together.

Flat (note) A half step lower than a natural tone. Flats and sharps are the black keys on a keyboard.

Fret One of a sequence of ridges across the fingerboard of a stringed instrument, such as a guitar.

Grime A genre of dance music with rapping over fast electronic beats (at around 130bpm).

Half step A semitone—half of a whole tone, the smallest interval between two notes in Western music.

Harmony A combination of notes played together to make chord sequences that sound pleasing.

Hymn A religious song of praise.

Jam (verb) A group of musicians making up music as they go along.

Melody Notes that have been arranged into a distinctive pattern or sequence. Also known as a tune.

Octave A repeating pattern of seven whole tones (or 12 semitones).

Opera A play set to music for singers accompanied by an orchestra.

Orchestra A large group of musicians playing different instruments together.

Overture A one-movement piece of music that can be used to introduce an opera or can be performed separately.

Phrase A short, distinctive passage of music.

Pitch How high or low a note is. To alter the pitch is to make a note higher or lower.

Plainsong A type of early European religious music, consisting of simple melodies sung in Latin, usually without harmonies or accompanying instruments.

Playback singer A singer who records songs for a movie soundtrack to be mimed by an actor on film.

Plectrum A thin, flat tool used to pluck or strum a stringed instrument.

Quintet A group of five musicians.

Ragtime A style of popular music with syncopated rhythm created by African-American musicians in the early 1900s.

Reed A piece of wood, cane, or metal that is made to vibrate in some instruments to produce sound.

Reformation A 16th-century religious movement that aimed to reform the Roman Catholic Church and resulted in the establishment of the Protestant churches.

Refrain A phrase or verse that is repeated regularly in a song.

Reggae A style of music originating from Jamaica, with a strong second and fourth beat.

Rhythm The pulse or feel (rather than the notes) of music, made up of repeated percussive patterns.

Sample A small portion of music from one song that is copied and used to create another song. Recording music like this is known as sampling.

Sanskrit An Indian language that is one of the oldest languages in the world.

Scale A set of notes based on the pattern of intervals between the notes.

Sharp (note) A half step higher than a natural tone. Flats and sharps are the black keys on a keyboard.

Sight-read To read and perform from sheet music without any preparation.

Spiritual A type of religious folk music associated with enslaved Africans in the American South.

Staff In musical notation, a staff is a set of five horizontal lines representing different pitches on which musical notes are written. Also called a stave.

Suite A set of instrumental pieces of music designed to be played in succession.

Swing A type of jazz music with a flowing, danceable rhythm, played by big bands of the 1930s and '40s.

Syncopation Changing the regular rhythm of a piece by emphasizing unusual or unexpected parts; stressing a beat that wouldn't normally be stressed.

Tempo The speed of a piece of music.

Virtuoso A musician who displays a high level of skill at singing or playing a particular instrument.

Further Reading & Resources

BOOKS FOR YOUNGER READERS

Children's Book of Music (DK)
Explores music from its beginnings to the technological developments of the modern age.

Concise Guide to Jazz, 7th Edition (Pearson)
Focusing on 50 historical figures, this book examines how jazz originated, how it is made, what to listen for, and the major style eras.

Hip Hop Around the World: An Encyclopedia (Greenwood)
Covers all aspects of international hip-hop as expressed through music, art, fashion, dance, and political activity.

Lives of the Musicians: Good Times, Bad Times (and What the Neighbors Thought)
(HMH Books for Young Readers)
The life stories of figures such as Mozart, Scott Joplin, Nadia Boulanger, and Woody Guthrie.

Musicals: The Definitive Illustrated Story (DK)
From Les Misérables and The Wizard of Oz to Disney and Mary Poppins, this book explores the history of musical theater. Infographics summarize plot, characters, and songs from the best loved musicals.

The Oxford Companion to Music
(Oxford University Press)
First published in 1938, this book offers authoritative information on all aspects of music. A helpful guide for students, teachers, performers, concertgoers, record collectors, and music lovers.

Story of the Orchestra: Listen While You Learn About the Instruments, the Music and the Composers Who Wrote the Music! (Black Dog & Leventhal)
An introduction to the world of classical music, from composers to instruments of the orchestra. With an accompanying 70-minute CD.

ONLINE RESOURCES AND PLACES TO VISIT IN PERSON

Alabama Jazz Hall of Fame
1701B 4th Avenue N
Birmingham, AL 35203
jazzhall.com

Includes exhibits related to Nat King Cole, Duke Ellington, and Lionel Hampton. It also holds jazz workshops for students.

American Jazz Museum
1616 E 18th Street
Kansas City, MO 64108
americanjazzmuseum.org

Explore the history of American jazz music, with exhibits on Duke Ellington, Charlie Parker, Ella Fitzgerald, and others, and a jazz club that holds live performances.

Country Music Hall of Fame
222 5th Ave S, Nashville, TN 37203
countrymusichalloffame.org

A museum dedicated to the history and interpretation of American country music. With interactive galleries and an online digital archive.

GRAMMY Museum L.A. Live
800 W Olympic Boulevard
Los Angeles, CA 90015
grammymuseum.org

An interactive museum devoted to the history and winners of the Grammy Awards.

The Metropolitan Museum of Art
1000 Fifth Avenue
New York, NY 10028
metmuseum.org

The museum's collection of instruments includes examples from 300 B.C. to the present.

Museum of Pop Culture
325 5th Avenue N
Seattle, WA 98109
mopop.org

Dedicated to contemporary popular culture, with interactive exhibits such as Sound Lab, where visitors can explore rock and roll instruments and perform music.

Musical Instrument Museum
4725 E Mayo Boulevard
Phoenix, AZ 85050
mim.org

Home to thousands of musical instruments from nearly 200 countries and territories, including ethnic, folk, and tribal music styles.

The National Music Museum
The University of South Dakota
414 East Clark Street
Vermillion, SD 57069
nmmusd.org

Includes over 15,000 American, European, and non-Western instruments from all cultures and historical periods. Has an online catalogue of musical instruments: emuseum.nmmusd.org

Rock and Roll Hall of Fame
1100 Rock and Roll Boulevard
Cleveland, Ohio 44114
rockhall.com

Showcases the past, present, and future of rock music, with videos of favorite performers, their costumes and guitars, and DJ recordings. With live shows and online archive resources.

Smithsonian Music
music.si.edu

Online recordings and podcasts related to music of many different genres from around the world.

STAX Museum of American Soul Music
926 E. McLemore Avenue
Memphis, TN 38106
staxmuseum.com

The history of American soul music with some 2,000 artifacts and interactive computer exhibits.

Yale University Collection of Musical Instruments
15 Hillhouse Avenue
New Haven, Connecticut 06511
collection.yale.edu

Features musical instruments through the ages, with audio tours and an online digital collection.

Index

Boldface indicates illustrations.

A

a cappella 171
A Tribe Called Quest 153, **153**
Academy Awards (Oscars) 81, 87, 113
acoustic guitars 78, **78,** 122, **122,** 128
Adé, King Sunny 159, **159**
Adele 157, **157**
African slaves 72, 89, 90, 91, 92, 93, 159
Afrika Bambaataa 161
Afro-Cuban music 110, 158, 159
Afrobeat 131, 158
Afropop 158-9
ambient house 162
American Civil War 58
American Idol TV show 172-3, **172-3**
American Revolutionary War 56, 57
amps/amplifiers 145, **145**
Anl, Adam 148, **148**
Apache Indian 136, **136**
arias 24
Armstrong, Louis 96, 97, **97,** 100, 102, 105, 107
art/artists and music 68, 71, 109, 127, 152
Asian opera **7,** 62-3, **62-3,** 65
Aztec 14, **14,** 31, 33

B

barbershop quartets 170, 171
Bach, Johann Sebastian 28, **28,** 29, 30
Baez, Joan 122, 123, **123**
bagpipes 15, **15**
Baker, Chet 106, **106**
Balinese gamelan 20-1, **20-1**
Ballets Russes 70, 71, **71**
ballets 55, 70-1, **70-1, 74,** 93
banjos 78, 92, 93, **93,** 96, 159
Baroque musical era 24-31, 33
barrel drums/dhol 137
Bartók, Béla 69
Basie, William "Count" 98
bass guitars 130, 142
Beach, Amy 52, 53, **53**
Beach Boys, The 126, 139, **139**
Beatles, The **7,** 30, 122, 124, 126-7, **126-7,** 132, 135, 170, 176
beats per minute (bpm) 163
bebop/bop 104-5, 106, 107, 109
Beethoven, Ludwig van 36, 37, 41, **42,** 42-3, 44, 45, 50
Beijing jingju (opera) **7,** 62-3, **62-3,** 65

Berlin, Irving 80, **80,** 82
Berlioz, Louis-Hector 45, **45**
Berry, Chuck 116, 120, **120,** 128, 145
Beyoncé 168, 169, **169**
bhangra 137, **137**
Bhosle, Asha 136, 137
Bieber, Justin 162, 176, 179
big band jazz 96, 98-103, 109, 112, 117
Big Bang 175, **175**
"Birth of Cool" recordings 106
Black Sabbath 144
Blondie 146
bluegrass 78, 79
blues 89, 94-5, 112, 113, 117, 128-9, 152, 157
Bolan, Marc 134
Bollywood 85, **85,** 136, 137
bone flutes 12, **12**
bossa nova 110, 111, 113
Bowie, David 134, **134,** 138, 139, **139,** 157, 160, 176
boy bands 170-1, 174
Brahms, Johannes 50, 51, 65, **65**
brass instruments 43, **43**
Brazilian Latin jazz 110-11
Bristow, George 57
British musical invasion (1960s) 126-7
Broadway musicals 76-7, **76-7,** 81
Brooks, Garth 166
Brown, James 118, 130, 131, **131,** 153
Brubeck, Dave 106, 107
Bruckner, Anton 50, **50,** 51
BTS 174, **174**
Buddhism 16, **16**
Byrd, William 22, 23

C

Caccini, Francesca 52
cakewalks 92, 93
Calloway, Cab 98, **98,** 102, 105
cantatas 28
cantillation 16
Carreño, Teresa 65, **65**
Carter Family 78, **78**
Cash, Johnny 78, 87, **87,** 167
cassette tapes 136, 137, **137**
Castelloza 15, **15**
chamber pieces 38, 40, **40,** 41, 47
chants 16, 17
Childish Gambino 176, **176**
China 12, 13, 62-3, 65
Chinai, Alisha 137
Chopin, Frédéric 47, **47,** 54, **54**
choral music 24, 57
chords 18
Christy, June 107, **107**

chromatic scale 9
church music 17, 26, **26,** 31, 90, 118, 171
civil rights movement 118, 119, 122, 123
Clapton, Eric 112, 113, 129, **129,** 145
clarinets 37, **37**
Clark, Petula 126, **126,** 127
Clash, The 146, **146**
Cline, Patsy 78, 166
Cobain, Kurt 149, **149**
Colemen, Ornette 108, **108**
Collins, Bootsy 130, **130**
Coltrane, John 108, 109, **109,** 110
concept albums 134, 135, 139
concertos 26, 27, 38
conductors 36, 49
cool jazz 106-7
Copland, Aaron 74, **74,** 75
cornets 96, 97, **97**
Cotton Club, Harlem 98, 99, 102
country music 78-9, 87, 120, 164, 166-7, 177
Cuban dance music 110
cumbia 73, **73**
cymbals 20, **20**

D

da Palestrina, Giovanni Pierluigi 22, 23, **23**
Daft Punk 161, 163, **163**
dancehall, Jamaican 142, 143
d'Arezzo, Guido 18
Dave Brubeck Quartet 107
Davis Jr., Sammy 82, 86, **86**
Davis, Miles 106, **106,** 107, **107,** 109
de Machaut, Guillaume 18, 19, **19**
de Romans, Bieiris 32
Debussy, Claude 68, **68,** 69
Deep Purple 144
Dekker, Desmond 142, **142**
Depeche Mode 148, 161, 162
Destiny's Child 168, 169
Diaghilev, Sergei 70, 71
Diddley, Bo 116, 117, **117**
digital audio workstation (DAW) 163, **163,** 178
disco music 130, 148, 163
dissonance, musical 68, 69
Dixie Chicks 166, **166**
djembe drums 9, 91, **91**
DJs 121, 143, 152, 153, 154, 162
Domino, Fats 116
Dorsey, Tommy and Jimmy 100, **100**
Drake 176, 178, **178**
drum and bass music 143
drum machines 160, 161, **161**

drums 14, **14,** 31, **31,** 36, 63, **63,** 91, **91,** 111, 130, 133, 137, 158, 159
dub 142, 143, 162
dubstep 143
Duran Duran 148
Dvořák, Antonín 57, **57,** 74
Dylan, Bob 122, 123, **123,** 167

E

Eagles, The 167
Egypt, ancient 12, 12, 13
1812 Overture (Tchaikovsky) 55
electric guitars 94, 116, 120, 121, **121,** 125, **125,** 128, **128,** 148, 149, 159
electronic dance music (EDM) 160, 162-3
electronic music 85, 107, 139, 146, 149 *see also* synthesizers
electropop 148, 162
Ellington, Duke 82, **88-9,** 89, 96, 98, 99, **99,** 104, 110
Elliott, Missy 152, 168, 169, **169**
Eno, Brian 160, **160**
Estefan, Gloria 150, 165, **165**

F

Farrenc, Louise 52, **52**
Federal Music Project 75
Fernandes, Gaspar 33
festivals 123, **123,** 179
Festspielhaus theatre, Bayreuth 61, **61**
Fiddlin' John Carson 78
Fields, Dorothy 81, **81**
Fischer, Johann 36
Fisk Jubilee Singers 90, **90**
Fitzgerald, Ella 82, **82,** 83
flamenco music/dancing 72, **72**
flutes 12, **12,** 37, **37**
folk music 9, 30, 40, 47, 53, 54, 57, 69, 71, 72, 74, 75, 78, 79, 90, 94, 142
folk revival, 1960s 122-3
folk rock 122, 145
The Four Seasons (A. Vivaldi) 27
Franklin, Aretha 118, 119, **119,** 150, **150**
free jazz 108-9
fugue 26
funk 130-1, 138, 153, 158, 163

G

gamelan orchestras 20-1, **20-1,** 69, **69**
garage music 162
Garfunkel, Art 122, **122**
Gaynor, Gloria 131
Geldof, Bob 157, **157**
Genesis 134, **134**
Germany 28-9, 50, 60, 61, 64, 65
Gershwin, George 74, 80, 82, 83, **83**
Gershwin, Ira 82, 83

Gilberto, João 111, **111,** 113, **113**
Gillespie, Dizzy 104, 105, **105,** 107, 110
Gilmore, Patrick 58
glam rock 134, 144
Glass, Philip 160
glissando 118
gongs 20, **20-1,** 21, 63
Goodman, Benny 100, **100,** 101
Gordy, Berry 118, **118**
gospel music 90, 117, 118-19, 120, 131, 179
Goth rock 139, 148, 149
Grammy Awards 83, 87, 90, 133, 136, 157, 159, 165, 167, 177, 181
Grand Ole Opry radio show 78, 79, **79,** 164
Grande, Ariana 168, 178, **178**
Grandmaster Flash, DJ 152
Great American Songbook 82-3
Great Depression 74, 75, 82, 98, 102
Greece, ancient 12, 13, 14, 29, 36
Grieg, Edvard 55
grunge 148, 149, 166
Guetta, DJ David 162
guitars 72, 73, **73,** 78, **78,** 79, **79,** 86, 94, 112, 113, 116, 117, **117,** 120, 121, **121,** 122, **122,** 128, **128,** 130, 145, 148, 149, 156, 159
guqin 43, **43**
Guthrie, Woody 122, 123

H

Habichuela, Pepe 72, **72**
Hammerstein II, Oscar 80, 87, **87**
Handel, George Frideric 24, 29, 30, 31, **31**
Handy, W. C. 91, **91,** 94, 95, 110
Harlem Renaissance 99, **99**
harmonicas 129, **129,** 138
harmony 9
harpsichords, 22, 30, **30**
Harriott, Joe 108, 110
Harris, Emmylou 167, **167**
Harris, Roy 74, 75, **75**
Harry, Debbie 146, **146**
Haydn, Joseph 36, 37, **37,** 39, 40, **40,** 44, 54
heavy metal 141, 144-5
Henderson, Fletcher 98, 100, **101**
Hendrix, Jimi 117, 123, **123,** 144, 145
Hermann, Bernard 84, 85, **85**
highlife music 138, 158
Hildegard of Bingen 32, **32**
Hindi pop 136, 137
Hindu music 14, **14,** 16, 33, 132, 136
hip-hop 73, 130, 141, 143, 152-5, 160, 161, 163, 168, 169, 181
Holiday, Billie **7,** 104, **104,** 105, **105**
Hooker, John Lee 117

hornpipes 15
house music 162
Houston, Whitney 150, 151, **151**
Howlin' Wolf 94
Huangmei opera 63, **63**
hymns 16, 17, 74, 75

I

Imagine Dragons 7, **7,** 181, **181**
improvisation 96, 97, 98, 104, 108-9
Inca 31
India 14, 16, 33, 54, 87, 110, 132, 133
indie rock 148, 163
Indipop 136-7
Indo-jazz fusion 110
instrumentals, Baroque 26
instrumentals, Renaissance 22
internet, influence of 178-9
Islamic music 16, 17, **17**
Italian Renaissance 22
Italy 24, 26, 33, 44, 50, 60, 61, 64
Ives, Charles 74, 75, **75**
Izumo no Okuni 62, 64, **64**

J

J-pop 175
Jackson 5 119, 164, 170, **170**
Jackson, Mahalia 118, 119, **119**
Jackson, Michael 164, **164,** 181
Jamaica 136, 137, 142, 143, 152, 162
Japan 22, 43, 62, 64, 135, 175
Jay-Z 152, **152,** 169
jazz 59, 74, 75, 83, 96-111, 113, 116, 126, 131, 132, 153, 158, 163
Jett, Joan 135, **135**
John, Elton 156, 157, **157**
Johnson, Robert 94, 95, 113, **113**
Jonas Brothers 170, 171, **171**
Joplin, Janis 123, 138, 139, **139**
Joplin, Scott 92, 93, **93**
Jordan, Louis 116, **116**
Judaism/Jewish music 16, 41

K

K-pop 174-5
kabuki 62, **62,** 64
Keita, Salif 158, 159, **159**
Kern, Jerome 80, 83
Keys, Alicia 169, **169**
Khan, Allauddin 132, 133
Kind of Blue (M. Davis) 107
King, B.B. 94, 112, **112,** 116
King Jr., Martin Luther 119, 138
King Oliver 96, **96**
KISS 144, **144**
klezmer music 41, **41**
Knight, Gladys 119
Knuckles, Frankie 162, **162**
Korngold, Erich 84, 84
Kouyaté, Bassekou 159
Kraftwerk 160, 161, **161,** 162

Kuti, Fela 131, 138, **138,** 158
kwela music 108, 109, 113

L
La Bohème (G. Puccini) 60, **60**
Lady Gaga **6,** 85, 140, **140,** 176, 179, **179**
Lamar, Kendrick 181, **181**
Latin American music 72, 73, 110–11
Lauper, Cyndi 150, **150**
Led Zeppelin 144, 145, **145**
Lennox, Annie 150, **150**
Lewis, John 106
librettos 63, 76
Liszt, Franz 46, 47, **47,** 51, 54, 58, 69
Little Richard 116, 120, **120**
Live Aid 157, **157**
London, England 31, 37, 80, 85, 108, 139
L'Orfeo (C. Monteverdi) 24
Louis XIV of France, King 25, 33
Lully, Jean-Baptiste 25, **25,** 33, **33**
lutes 14, 15, 22, **23,** 63, 73
Luther, Martin 17, **17**
lyres **6,** 12, 13, **13**

M
Mabaso, Lemmy 109, **109**
MacDowell, Edward 56, **56**
Machito and His Afro-Cubans 110, **110**
Madonna 150, 151, **151,** 157, 162, 168
madrigals 22, 23
The Magice Flute (Mozart) 38, **38**
Mahler, Gustav 50, 51, **51**
Makeba, Miriam 158
mambo 110, 111
mandolins 63, **63,** 79
Mangeshkar, Lata 137, **137**
Marley, Bob 142, 143, **143**
Mars, Bruno 7, 176, 177, **177,** 181, **181**
Masekela, Hugh 158
Mashiyane, Spokes 109, 113
Maya 10–11, 31
Mayer, John 110
medieval India 14
Mei Lanfang 65, **65**
melisma 118, 151
melody 9
Mendelssohn, Fanny 53, **53**
Mendelssohn, Felix 45, 53
Mendes, Shawn 179, **179**
Menudo 170
Mercury, Freddie 134
merengue 110
metallophones 20, **20,** 21, **21**
military/marching bands 58, **58,** 59, 117
Miller, Glenn 100, 101, **101**
minimalism 160

minstrel shows 91
Moby 163, **163**
Monáe, Janelle 180, **180**
Monk, Thelonius 104, **104**
Monkees, The 126, 134, 170, 171
Monroe, Bill 79, **79**
Monteverdi, Claudio 24, **24**
Morning Musume 175, **175**
Morton, Jelly Roll 96, 97, 110
mosques 17, **17**
Motörhead 145
Motown record label 118, **118,** 119, **119,** 138, 170
movie scores 84–5, 87, 93, 130, 163
Mozart, Wolfgang Amadeus 7, 37, 38–9, **39,** 40, 41, 42, 44, 60
Muddy Waters 94, 95, **95**
muezzin 17, **17**
Muhammad, Ali Shadeed 152
Muslims 16, **16,** 132

N
Nashville, Tennessee 78–9, 166, 167
Nationalist movement 54–7, 69, 72
N'Dour, Youssou 158, **158**
Neruda, Wilma 46, **46**
New Orleans, Louisiana 96, 97, 110, 116, 119
New Romantics 139, 148
new wave 139, 146
New World Symphony (A. Dvořák) 57
New York City 76–7, 81, 83, 92, 98, 99, 102, 104, 105, 147, 152, 162
ngoni 159, **159**
Nijinsky, Vaslav 71
Nirvana 148, 149
notation, musical 18, 24
notes, musical 9, **9,** 19, **19**
*NSYNC, 171, **171**
nu metal 144
The Nutcracker (Tchaikovsky) 55

O
O-Town 171, 172
octaves 8
"Ode to Joy" (Beethoven) 43
One Direction 170, **170,** 171, 172
operas 24, 25, 29, 31, 38, 52, 55, 60–1, 62–3, 64, 65, 71, 80, 93
orchestras 20–1, **20–1,** 24, 26, **34,** 36, **36,** 47, 48–9, **48–9,** 51, 57, 69, **69,** 98, 102–3, **102–3,** 107
organs 28, 29, **29,** 84, 85, **85,** 163
Original Dixieland Jazz Band 98
Osibisa 158, **158**
overtures 25

P
Paganini, Niccolò 46, **46,** 47, 73
Paine, John Knowles 56, 57, **57**

panpipes 31, **31**
Paris, France 47, 52, 70
Parker, Charlie 104, 105, **105**
Parton, Dolly 78, 164, **164,** 166
Pastoral (Beethoven) 44, 45
patrons, musical 25, 47
Patsy, Cline 78
Pavlova, Anna 132
pentatonic scale 68
percussion instruments 48, 111
Perry, Katy 168, 179, **179**
Perry, Lee "Scratch" 143, **143**
Pet Sounds (The Beach Boys) 139
Peter and the Wolf (S. Prokofiev) 71, **71**
pianos/pianists 36, 38, 39, **39,** 47, 51, 52, 53, 64, 65, 71, 75, 83, 84, 92, 97, 103, 104, 106, 116, 119, 157
Pink Floyd 135, **135**
pipe organs 29, **29,** 85, **85**
pitch and frequency 8, 18, 24, 118
Pixies 148, **148**
plainsong 16, 17, **17,** 18
Pollock, Jackson 109, **109**
polyphony 17
Porter, Cole 80, 81, **81,** 83
preludes 31
Presley, Elvis 7, 120, 121, **121**
Prince 176, **176**
prog rock 134–5, 145
program music 45, 51
Prokofiev, Sergei 71, 84
protest folk music 122, 123
Psy 175, **175**
Puccini, Giacomo 60, 61, **61,** 70
Puente, Ernesto "Tito" 111, **111**
punk rock 139, 146–7, **147,** 149
Purcell, Henry 25, **25**
Pythagoras 13, **13**

Q
Queen 134, 156, 157
Queen Latifah 168, **168**

R
racism 95, 99, 101, 117, 118
radio 78, 79, 101, 121, 166
ragas 133
ragga 142
ragtime music 92–3
Ramones 146, 147, **147**
rap 136, 137, 143, 152, 154, 168, 169, 175, 181
Ravel, Maurice 71, 72
Ray, Satyajit 87, **87**
Red Hot Chili Peppers 165, **165**
Red Hot Peppers 97
Reformation 17
reggae 136, 142–3, 146, 163
religious rituals, early 12, 14, **16–17,** 16–21, **20–1,** 32

Renaissance 22–3
Reynolds, Dan 181, **181**
rhythm 8, 18, 163
rhythm and blues (R&B) 116–17, 118, 120, 128, 131, 168, 170, 180
Rihanna 168, 176, 180, **180**
Rimsky-Korsakov, Nikolay 71
Ring Cycle (R. Wagner) 61
Robinson, Smokey 119
rock and roll 82, 116, 119, 120–1, 128, 157
Rock and Roll Hall of Fame 87, 129, 147
rock operas 127
rockabilly 78
Rodgers, Jimmie 78, **78**
Rodgers, Richard 80, 87, **87**
Rogers, Kenny 166
Roland TR-808 161, **161**
Rolling Stones, The 126, 128, **128,** 129, 132, 156
Romans 14, 15
Romantic musical tradition 42–7, 54, 60, 134
Ross, Diana **118,** 119
Rossini, Gioachino 60, **60**
rota (singing in the round) 19, **19**
Roxy Music 134, 160
Ruddick, Osbourne "King Tubby" 143
Run-DMC 152, 154–5, **154–5,** 157
Russia 55, 70

S
Saint-Saëns, Camille 84
salsa 110
Salt-N-Pepa 168
samba 110, 111
sampling 153, 161
sarabande 31, **31**
Saturday Night Fever 130, **130**
saxophones 117, **117**
Scarlatti, Alessandro 25
Scarlatti, Domenico 30, **30**
Schoenberg, Arnold 68, 69, **69,** 71
Schubert, Franz 40, **40,** 41, **41,** 45
Schumann, Clara 51, **51,** 53
Segovia, Andrés 73, 86, **86**
segregation, racial 95, 99, 117
Seo Taiji and Boys 174
Sgt. Pepper's Lonely Hearts Club Band (The Beatles) 135, **135**
Shankar, Ravi 132, 133, **133**
Sheeran, Ed **156,** 176
Simon, Paul 122, **122**
Sinatra, Frank 82, **82,** 86, 100, 112
Siouxsie and the Banshees 146, 147, **147**
sitars 132–3, **132–3**
ska 142, 143
skiffle 126

Slave Songs of the United States 90, 91, **91**
slaves 72, 73, 89, 90, 91, 92, 93, 159
Smetana, Bedrich 55
Smith, Bessie 91, 94, 95, **95,** 99, 105
Smith, Mamie 94, **94**
The Smiths 148
social media 178, 179
sonatas 37, **37,** 41
Songwriters Hall of Fame 81, 87, 169
soul music 117, 118–19, 130, 131, 153, 159
Soul Train TV show 131, **131**
Sousa, John Philip 58–9, **59**
sousaphone 59, **59**
South Africa 108, 109, 113
Soviet Union 71, 108
see also Russia
Spain 30, 72, 110
Spears, Britney 165, **165**
Spice Girls 168, **168**
spirituals, African-American 90, 91, 118
Spotify 178, **178**
Springsteen, Bruce 124–5, **124–5**
stadium concerts 124–5, **124–5,** 156–7
staff paper/staves 18, 19, 23
Stax records 118
steel guitars 78, 79, **79**
Stradivari, Antonio 27
Stravinsky, Igor 70, 71, **71**
streaming music 178
string quartets 40, 41
Strozzi, Barbara 52, **52**
Sun Ra 108
Swan Lake (Tchaikovsky) 55
Swift, Taylor 7, 166, 177, **177**
swing 100–1, 104, 112, 120
symphonic poems 50, 51
symphonies 36, 37, 42, 44, 45, 50, 51, 53, 57, 65, 74, 75
Symphony No. 5 in C Minor (Beethoven) 42
Symphony No. 6 in F major (Beethoven) 45
Symphony No. 9 (Beethoven) 43, 50
syncopation 68, 92, 118
synthesizers 6, 148, 149, **149,** 153, 160, 161, 163

T
Tagore, Rabindranath 54
talking drums 159
Talking Heads 146–7
Tallis, Thomas 23
Tansen, Mian 33, **33**
Tchaikovsky, Pyotr Ilyich 55, **55**
techno 162, 163
Telemann, Georg Philip 29, **29**
tempo 163
Tin Pan Alley 83, **83**

Toccata and Fugue in D Minor (J. S. Bach) 28
trobairitz 15, **15,** 32, **32**
trombones 22, 43, **43,** 101
troubadours 15, 32
trumpets 14, 36, 97, 104, 105, 106, 107, 158
Turner, Tina 156, 157
TV talent shows 172–3, **172–3**
12-bar blues 95, 120
Tympany Five 116, **116**

U
U2 112, 156, **156,** 157
United Service Organization (USO) 101
Uragami Gyokudo 43
Urban, Keith 167, **167**
U.S. Marine Band 58, 59

V
van Halen, Eddie 145, **145**
Venice, Italy 26, 27
Verdi, Giuseppe 64, **64,** 69
videos, music 85, 177, 179
Vienna, Austria 36, 38, 39, **39,** 41, 47, 69
Vietnam 72, 73, 122
violins/violinists 27, **27,** 36, 46, 47, 48, 68, 110, 117
virginals 22, **22**
virtuosi 46–7, 51, 52, 73, 97, 98, 132, 176
Vivaldi, Antonio 26, 27, **27**
von Weber, Carl Maria 60

W
Wagner, Richard 60, 61, **61,** 65, 69
Whiteman, Paul 96, 98, **98**
Who, The 25, 126, 127, **127**
Wicked musical 76–7, **76–7**
Williams, Ralph Vaughan 69
Wilson, Brian 138, 139
women's rights 53, 64, 65, 150, 151, 168–9
Wonder, Stevie 119, 129, **129,** 138, **138**
Woodstock festival 123, **123**
woodwinds 36, 37, **37**
Wurlitzer organs 85, **85**

Y
The Yardbirds 128, 129
yellow music 73
Young, Neil 166, 167

Illustration Credits

Since 1888, the National Geographic Society has funded more than 12,000 research, exploration, and preservation projects around the world. The Society receives funds from National Geographic Partners, LLC, funded in part by your purchase. A portion of the proceeds from this book supports this vital work. To learn more, visit natgeo.com/info.

NATIONAL GEOGRAPHIC and Yellow Border Design are trademarks of the National Geographic Society, used under license.

For more information, visit nationalgeographic.com, call 1-877-873-6846, or write to the following address:

National Geographic Partners
1145 17th Street N.W.
Washington, DC 20036-4688 U.S.A.

Visit us online at nationalgeographic.com/books

For librarians and teachers: ngchildrensbooks.org

More for kids from National Geographic: natgeokids.com

National Geographic Kids magazine inspires children to explore their world with fun yet educational articles on animals, science, nature, and more. Using fresh storytelling and amazing photography, *Nat Geo Kids* shows kids ages 6 to 14 the fascinating truth about the world—and why they should care. **kids.nationalgeographic.com/subscribe**

For information about special discounts for bulk purchases, please contact National Geographic Books Special Sales: specialsales@natgeo.com

For rights or permissions inquiries, please contact National Geographic Books Subsidiary Rights: bookrights@natgeo.com

Cover design by Amanda Larsen and Carlton Books Limited

Design, Editorial, and Production by Carlton Books Limited

The publisher would like to acknowledge the following people for making this book possible: Becky Baines, vice president and editorial director; Shelby Lees, senior editor; Michaela Weglinski, project editor; Catherine Frank, text editor; Lori Epstein, photo director; Amanda Larsen, design director; Joan Gossett, editorial production manager; Anne LeongSon and Gus Tello, design production assistants; and Nicole Overton, for her review of the book.

Library of Congress Cataloging-in-Publication Data

Names: National Geographic Kids (Firm) author.
Title: Turn it up! / by National Geographic Kids.
Description: Washington, DC : National Geographic Kids, [2019] | Includes index.
Identifiers: LCCN 2018035848| ISBN 9781426335419 (hardcover) | ISBN 9781426335426 (hardcover)
Subjects: LCSH: Music--History and criticism--Juvenile literature.
Classification: LCC ML3928 .N37 2019 | DDC 780.9--dc23
LC record available at https://lccn.loc.gov/2018035848

Printed in China
19/PPS/1